At Issue

The U.S. Policy on Cuba

Other Books in the At Issue Series:

At Issue

The U.S. Policy on Cuba

Amy Francis, Book Editor

GREENHAVEN PRESS
A part of Gale, Cengage Learning

GALE
CENGAGE Learning™

Detroit • New York • San Francisco • New Haven, Conn • Waterville, Maine • London

Christine Nasso, *Publisher*
Elizabeth Des Chenes, *Managing Editor*

© 2009 Greenhaven Press, a part of Gale, Cengage Learning.

Cover photograph © Images.com/Corbis.

LIBRARY OF CONGRESS CATALOGING-IN-PUBLICATION DATA

The U.S. Policy on Cuba / Amy Francis, book editor.
   p. cm. -- (At issue)
   Includes bibliographical references and index.
   ISBN 978-0-7377-4108-7 (hardcover)
   ISBN 978-0-7377-4109-4 (pbk.)
   1. Economic sanctions, American--Cuba--Juvenile literature. 2. Cuba--Foreign economic relations--United States--Juvenile literature. 3. United States--Foreign economic relations--Cuba--Juvenile literature. I. I. Francis, Amy. II. II. Title: United States policy on Cuba.
   HF1500.5.U5U53 2009
   382.0973'07291--dc22
                                                        2008030534

Printed in the United States of America
1 2 3 4 5 6 7 12 11 10 09 08

Contents

Introduction

Although there is widespread international recognition that human rights are being violated in Cuba, the United States has received little support from the international community for its policies on the island just 90 miles off the coast of Florida. The lack of international support makes it harder for the United States to enforce its policies, and some critics believe this makes the conditions in Cuba even worse. According to Joe Vivanco at Human Rights Watch, "Because the embargo is bitterly opposed by most nations, it enables the Cuban government to divide the international community, leading, ironically, to less international pressure on Fidel Castro, not more."

For example, in October 2007, the General Assembly at the United Nations voted 184 to 4 in favor of the United States ending the trade embargo. This vote was followed quickly by the adoption of a resolution stating that the U.S. embargo caused harm to "the Cuban people and Cuban nationals living in other countries." Castro was quick to distribute this news within Cuba as evidence that the United States was to blame for the country's problems. Although Ronald Goddard, speaking on behalf of the United States at the General Assembly, countered that it was Cuba's own policies that negatively affected human rights in Cuba and not U.S. policy, the United States once again received a clear message that the United Nations did not support the U.S. embargo against Cuba.

The European Union (EU), a group with twenty-seven member states formed to improve political and economic relationships, has also been critical of the U.S. policy on Cuba. In an EU Presidency Statement released in 2005 on the issues of "ending the economic, commercial and financial embargo imposed by the United States of America against Cuba," the EU expressed serious concern over human rights abuses in

Cuba but added that the EU believes "the lifting of the U.S. trade embargo would open Cuba's economy to the benefit of the Cuban people."

Although it does not prohibit trade, the EU does impose some sanctions against Cuba. After Fidel Castro resigned and his brother Raul assumed the office of the President of Cuba in February 2008, many members of the EU expressed belief that the time had come to completely end sanctions. These debates are ongoing. Spain in particular favors lifting all sanctions, but some members of the EU are resisting, including the Czech Republic, which is leading a group of former communist states in opposition. The United States and a number of human rights organizations object to the end of sanctions by the EU.

In addition to justifying its policy on Cuba by pointing to human rights violations, the United States also includes Cuba on the State Department's list of state sponsors of terror, along with Iran, North Korea, Syria, Sudan, and Libya. The U.S. State Department reports that that "Cuba actively continued to oppose the U.S.-led Coalition prosecuting the global war on terror and has publicly condemned various U.S. policies and actions."

The inclusion of Cuba on this list has come under heavy scrutiny both at home and abroad. Author and former U.S. diplomat Wayne S. Smith states that Cuba "does not endorse terrorism, as the State Department says it does" and points out that Cuba "has signed all twelve UN anti-terrorist resolutions and offered to sign agreements with the United States to cooperate in combating terrorism."

Venezuela has sharply criticized the United States as being hypocritical in its stance on terrorism since the U.S. has not granted Venezuela's request for an extradition of Cuban-born Venezuelan Luis Posada. Posada is wanted on charges of blowing up a Cuban airline in 1976, numerous deadly bombings on tourist sites in Cuba in 1997, and an assassination attempt on Fidel Castro in 2000. Although the United Nations Security Council stated in 2001 that "countries should not give safe haven or any kind of assistance to people involved in present or past terrorist activities," an immigration judge ruled in 2005 that Posada could not be extradited because he faced torture in Venezuela. The 2005 Ibero-American Summit, an annual forum sponsored by the Iberoamerican Community of Nations, also resulted in a demand for the man "responsible for the terrorist blowing-up of a plane of Cubana Aviation in October 1976" to be brought to justice. Despite these statements, the United States continues to allow Posada to remain in the country.

With or without international support, the question of the effectiveness of the U.S. policy on Cuba is frequently disputed within the United States. The extent to which the U.S. policy is effective is explored by the authors in *At Issue: U.S. Policy on Cuba.*

1

The United States Needs to Do More to Help the Cuban People

Margot Adler

Margot Adler is a National Public Radio correspondent and host of Justice Talking. Nicholás Gutiérrez is a member of the Cuba Legal Transition Committee of the Cuban American Bar Association. Julia Sweig is the director of the Latin American Studies Program at the Council on Foreign Relations.

The U.S. policy on Cuba is not effective. While the U.S. claims sanctions against Cuba will eliminate suffering for people living on the island, the sanctions are being used by the Cuban government to justify oppression. Whether the ineffectiveness of the U.S. policy in Cuba is due to insufficient enforcement of the policy or flaws in the policy itself is a matter of intense debate. Either way, the United States needs to play a larger role in improving the future for Cubans. Now that Raul Castro is in power, the United States has a particularly important window of opportunity to act.

Versailles, a Cuban restaurant and coffee bar in Miami, Florida serves up the traditional café con leche to a politically spirited crowd of Cuban-Americans. Conversation about the future of U.S. relations with Cuba is commonplace among the people who gather here. We asked them what they thought of the embargo.

Margot Adler, "The Cuban Embargo: Should U.S. Policy Change? Interview with Nicholás Gutiérrez and Julia Sweig," *Justice Talking*, NPR, August 13, 2007. Copyright © 1999–2008 Annenberg Public Policy Center, University of Pennsylvania. Reproduced by permission.

Unidentified Female: I think the Cuban embargo doesn't make a difference. It only hurts the Cuban people. It doesn't hurt the Cuban government. It makes it more difficult for Cubans to get the things they need like medicines or things they would normally get from the United States. But it doesn't make a difference. It doesn't hurt the Cuban government. They still have dollars and they still, um—the Cuban government is not suffering, just the Cuban people. So I don't agree with the Cuban embargo. It's not really fulfilling the purpose that it originally had. So I think it should be lifted.

Unidentified Male: It doesn't matter what we do here. The embargo is in some way helping the Cuban government to stay in the way that they are because still the country is hidden from the public opinion. That's number one. Number two: If we open the embargo we probably will give more dollars to them. But at the same time, if we open the embargo they are going to be flooded with the American culture, the democratic way of life. There are going to be thousands of tourists that will go there and the Cuban people will learn more of what is in the open.

Unidentified Female: I think that there shouldn't be an embargo. That's how I feel. I think, um, capitalism works. I believe in that. And I think, I think the only people suffering are the Cubans. I'm totally against the embargo.

Unidentified Male: But I don't believe that. The government has been using and doing commercial business with everybody. So the embargo is something like . . . a word. To me, it's just a word. It's not an embargo.

Unidentified Male: I think it should stick because I don't feel that we should do anything for the better of communism, for the better of Castro. I think they should stick with it and do it even more hard than what it is now. Don't let nothing go in or out of Cuba. Nothing. Nothing.

The Failure of U.S. Policy and Effect of the Embargo

Margot Adler: To debate whether or not the U.S. embargo should be lifted are Nicolás Gutiérrez and Julia Sweig. Nicolás is a lawyer in Miami and a member of the Cuba Legal Transition Committee of the Cuban American Bar Association. Julia is a senior fellow and director of the Latin American Studies Program at the Council on Foreign Relations. . . . The transfer of power from Fidel Castro to his younger brother Raul just over a year ago was a smooth one. Predicted unrest and a mass exodus of refugees did not materialize. Julia, does this show that U.S. policy toward Cuba has been a complete failure?

Julia Sweig: Well, yes it does. The regime-change policy as articulated just a couple of weeks before Fidel Castro turned over power provisionally to his brother was quite explicitly to interrupt the succession plans of the Castro brothers and to bring about a democratic transition through a variety of means. And that language sounds pretty soft by comparison to the way that same policy over the last 50 years has been articulated. The United States has been after overthrowing that regime since practically before Fidel Castro even took power. And it has been an abject failure as the last year has shown stable—pretty much business-as-usual on the island.

Nick, do you think U.S. sanctions and the embargo have been effective?

If you speak to any Cubans on the island today, nobody believes Fidel Castro's lies and promises after almost 49 years in power.

Nicolas Gutiérrez: Yes, they have, Margot, to the extent that they have been applied. In other words, Castro has been effectively isolated internationally. They would have a much greater effect had they been fully enforced. Let's remember that the embargo was never intended to be an end in and of itself. It was certain—it was only a means, a blunt instrument designed to be used in conjunction with other pro-democracy U.S. policies. And if there's any criticism of the Bush administration it's for not going far enough.

Castro's Credibility

Before I turn to Julia, let me ask you this, Nick: Doesn't the U.S. embargo allow the Cuban government to maintain popularity as an embattled tiny nation, you know, the sardine against the shark, fighting the military might of the greatest nation on earth?

Gutiérrez: No, Margot. I mean that's, with all due respect, almost nonsensical. If you speak to any Cubans on the island today, nobody believes Fidel Castro's lies and promises after almost 49 years in power. By now he's a laughing stock. So if the embargo didn't exist—and of course Fidel Castro would gain great international credibility if it were lifted—he would invent some other pretense, some other excuse to be in power. The Cuban people don't listen to Fidel Castro anymore. They're just subject to a totalitarian repressive security apparatus which does not allow them to engage in the normal political activity that anybody else in the world enjoys. Indeed you can't really speak about the U.S. embargo against Cuba without addressing the other embargo. And by the other embargo I mean the internal embargo that Fidel Castro has imposed on his own people, systematically denying them of all basic rights and liberties enjoyed by people elsewhere in the world.

Sweig: I would just say that to say that Cuba or Castro is isolated is wrong. They have trade and diplomatic ties with over 150 countries right now. Cuba can pick and choose who it has—whose capital comes in, but in terms of isolation, U.S. policy has failed to accomplish that. The second thing is that the nationalism that is inherent in Cuba's history and in the

Cuban people that well precedes Fidel Castro is absolutely heightened by the perception that because of U.S. policies Cuba is aggrieved and is the victim, and is the David to our Goliath. So I just want to say that we absolutely do reinforce that nationalism with these policies, as ineffective as they are.

> *The United States right now has no influence, no leverage, no effective way of affecting what is happening inside of Cuba.*

The Future of U.S. Relations with Cuba

Raul Castro just made a speech saying he's considering opening up the country to greater foreign investment. Is this the time to engage with Cuba, Julia?

Sweig: Well, I think absolutely this is the time to engage, because it is clear that Raul Castro is aware that he cannot deliver the bread-and-butter basic needs of the Cuban population with charisma and repression alone. One, he doesn't have the charisma, and two, the repressive apparatus is not as fully functional as it would have to be in order to deal with the heightened expectations of the Cuban people and their enormous pent-up demand for a better life. The United States right now has no influence, no leverage, no effective way of affecting what is happening inside of Cuba. So today, as Cuba does make this transition, is the moment. It doesn't mean sitting down and negotiating, our president to Raul Castro, whoever that president is, but it surely means freshening up our Rolodex, figuring out who is running those ministries, who's coming into office, who is in the second and third generation of individuals in Cuba in the economy, in the military, in various walks of life, that do see a future beyond the Castro brothers, and understand that because there are 11 million Cubans living in our country and because of geography and history, we're pretty much stuck with one another. So I absolutely think that there are ways to engage that are in the U.S. national interest. And we ought to start now.

Nick, how would you respond to that?

Gutiérrez: Well, precisely because Cuba can trade with the rest of the world, their argument that their people suffering is caused by the embargo is further undermined. Their people suffering is caused by the centralized command economy.

Sweig: I didn't say their suffering was because of the embargo. I said there is reason to engage that has to do with the U.S. national interests and having an influence on that future in Cuba whether it's economic or political or however it takes shape.

Gutiérrez: But Julia, what you fail to recognize is that future—that freshening of the Rolodex, as you put it—those relationships should be being made now not with the isolated, illegitimate, unelected, totalitarian regime and its top leaders but to the people. Section 109 of the Helms-Burton law [law enacted in 1996 which strengthened the U.S. embargo against Cuba], for example, authorizes and indeed encourages people-to-people contact, as did the Torricelli bill [bill proposed in 1992 to further strengthen the U.S. embargo] before it—dissidents—

Sweig: But in the context of things, "Hey, Cuban government, we want to overthrow you but let us have contact with your people"—

The Cuban American Community

Let me turn to another issue right here. Nick, you represent older Cuban Americans who fled Cuba after the revolution whose land was seized by the Cuban government. Cuban exiles who live in Miami are often painted in the press as extreme and irrational in their hard-line stance against Cuba. You represent hundreds of Cuban Americans. How would you describe this community?

Gutiérrez: Well, first of all, they're not all older because the older ones have children and grandchildren. In fact, I am a second-generation Cuban American. We're not pushing for any type of right-wing or extremist agenda. We're simply pushing for such radical notions—and I use that term sarcastically—as democracy, the rule of law, people having sovereignty over their own country and selecting their own leaders. These are not radical proposals.

Let's allow the open society that is the United States of America and our values to actually make way down there and affect Cuba directly.

Human Rights in Cuba

So let me ask two questions, one to each of you, that sort of deal in these issues. In Cuba there's no freedom of the press, there's no freedom of assembly. There are, you know, only limited elections, as you were talking about. There are political prisoners sitting in Cuban jails. If we lift the U.S. sanctions, Julia, aren't we essentially legitimizing an oppressive government?

Sweig: Yes and no. This has been a political objective, a policy objective of Fidel Castro, for as long as our sanctions have been in place, to get them lifted, at least in terms of what he says he wants. What they really want is a different matter. So it would potentially look like we're making a big concession to the dictator, but we would not be doing that for a very important reason, which is that the external calculus for Raul Castro right now is very, very easy. He and the cast of characters around him know exactly what to anticipate when it comes to the United States. If we really want to pose a challenge in this time of transition we will unilaterally say: You know what? Let's just go for it. Let's talk. Let's begin ties. Let's allow the open society that is the United States of America and our values to actually make way down there and affect Cuba directly. That's why the answer is also no, because it would pose an enormous challenge to the status quo internally in Cuba and lift the Cuban population's expectations of its own government to take advantage of the opening the United States represents.

Ordinary Cubans will tell you that their healthcare system is a shambles, that if you go to a hospital you have to bring your own lightbulb.

Now I want to turn to Nick and ask you: Are we as Americans projecting our notions about individual liberties onto Cuba? Hasn't Cuba made a choice that, let's say, education, housing, healthcare, are basic human rights that in their view are more important than free speech and freedom of the press? And isn't that their choice?

Gutiérrez: Margot, your question betrays a lack of touch with the reality in Cuba. If you talk to ordinary Cubans—I'm not talking about Communist Party hierarchy, I'm not talking about foreign investors—ordinary Cubans will tell you that their healthcare system is a shambles, that if you go to a hospital you have to bring your own lightbulb, your own sheets, your own sutures, that their education system is based on forced channelization into specialties that the regime wants where you don't get paid the money yourself, your salaries, it goes through the regime but then pays you a pittance in pesos. You have to, you have to quote-unquote "work voluntarily in the sugar fields" to pay for your education. So I mean that's just nonsense. Cuba has no independent economic sector. So if you lift the embargo, as Julia says, well that'll put a stress on the system. If you lift the embargo, who would American companies deal with in Cuba? They cannot deal with ordinary Cubans. They have to by definition deal with Cuban state agencies.

Sweig: Kind of like we do in China.

Comparing U.S. Policy in China and Cuba

Let's look at China for a minute. Is China a useful example? Here's an oppressive government, limited human rights for its citizens, a booming economy which the U.S. does business with but the business you could argue, Julia, hasn't helped democracy there. So what's the lesson for Cuba policy?

Sweig: I am not saying that we lift the embargo and you get democracy tomorrow in Cuba at all. I don't think that's the case. There's a very limited history of republican democracy in Cuba before the revolution. But what I am saying is that the fact of our policy puts an enormous constraint on the body politic's ability to have a conversation about what kind of future they are going to have. Because the regime manipulates our policy to restrict that conversation. So, no, of course China isn't the model, but I think we ought to take ourselves out of Cuba's domestic politics. Right now we're a huge player indirectly.

The U.S.—Oh, go on, very brief response.

Gutiérrez: Talk about arrogance and condescension. We're going to condemn the Cuban people to such a gradual transition that in China 34 years after the Nixon opening, or 35 years after the Nixon opening, they're still a totalitarian Communist regime that's responsible for Tiananmen Square, etc. And even with China opening economic policies somewhat, Raul and Fidel have yet to open anything like China or even Vietnam has done economically.

Cuba's Future

Okay, so here's my last question to both of you. In 10 years, after Fidel Castro and most likely Raul Castro are both gone, what do you see as the future of Cuba? We'll start with you Julia.

Sweig: I see a cautious society that will want to move on the economic reform front much faster than opening politically. I don't see a rapid transformation. I see a slow process of economic opening and a process in which the Communist

Party may begin to allow some of the very vibrant debates that happen behind closed doors manifest more openly. I don't see a multi-party system, but I do see more of an opening economically. Having said that, should the United States follow my advice, I do think that we could anticipate more rapid change because there will be a clamor for more of an opening if we take the first steps not from the regime but from the Cuban people.

Nick? The future in 15 or so years.

Gutiérrez: What I see, I'm less pessimistic than Julia. I see Eastern Europe; I see the Czech Republic; I see Slovakia; I see Lithuania, Latvia, and Estonia; I see Eastern Germany: all examples where a radical break from the communist past was implemented, where properties were returned in large part to the legitimate owners, where the rule of law was restored. I want to see, Margot, the entrepreneurial energies of Cuban people, which I share Julia's assessment on, unchained. And I think a system of rule of law and multi-party democracy that unchains that energy will unleash a potential that has not been seen in Latin America ever.

Nicolás Gutiérrez is a lawyer in Miami. He is leading legal efforts by hundreds of Cuban Americans who want to reclaim property that the Cuban government seized during the revolution. Julia Sweig is a senior fellow and director of the Latin American Studies Program at the Council on Foreign Relations. Her latest book is Friendly Fire: Losing Friends and Making Enemies in the Anti-American Century.

2

The Embargo Harms Both U.S. and Cuban Students

Cliff DuRand and Mike McGuire

Cliff Durand is a retired Professor of Philosophy at Morgan State University and former visiting professor at the University of Havana. He is co-founder of the Center for Global Justice. Mike McGuire is a global justice activist and translator.

According to the U.S. Supreme Court, travel cannot be made illegal, yet travel to Cuba is severely restricted by the U.S. embargo. Although students were previously exempt from the restrictions that eliminated tourist travel, they no longer have this right. Not only were educational travel licenses eliminated, researchers and other academics are also finding it increasingly difficult to obtain travel licenses. The result is that students and researchers in both the United States and Cuba are missing out on important exchanges of information, particularly in the areas of biotechnology and archeology, where researchers in Cuba are engaging in important work. Meanwhile the U.S. Congress and a growing number of Cuban Americans are against the embargo, and enforcing the embargo is tying up the same government resources assigned to enforce sanctions against terrorist networks and drug traffickers. The travel restrictions are causing a lot of harm and little, if any, benefit.

For forty-five years, the U.S. government has imposed a far-reaching embargo against its nearest neighbor in the Caribbean. It is the longest-standing and most extensive of the

Cliff Durand and Mike McGuire, "U.S. Embargo Walls Us In," *Academe*, September–October, 2004. Reproduced by permission.

many embargoes the United States maintains. It has erected an iron curtain between its citizens and those of Cuba, claiming that Cuba is an enemy. Any financial transactions with Cuba have been defined as "trading with the enemy." Although the U.S. Supreme Court has held that travel cannot be made illegal, the spending of U.S. dollars for travel to Cuba has been banned. Enforced by the Treasury Department, this embargo prohibits trade and travel except that licensed by the department's Office of Foreign Assets Control (OFAC).

Travel: A Right or a Privilege?

Only limited categories of people can be licensed to travel to Cuba—among them diplomats, journalists, and scholars. Travel by ordinary citizens for tourism is prohibited so as to deny Cuba access to U.S. dollars. For a long time, academics had been able to travel for research, professional conferences, or other educational activities. Students had sometimes been able to travel as well.

OFAC regulations and enforcement have varied from year to year, depending on the political winds in Washington and Florida. In January 2004, OFAC eliminated the people-to-people educational licenses that had permitted an estimated 40,000 ordinary tourists and students to travel to Cuba for educational programs even if they were not receiving academic credit. As a result, even before the new regulations, students had found it increasingly difficult to get authorization to travel.

Now even scholars are finding it harder to attend professional conferences in Cuba. In March, OFAC blocked over seventy-five U.S. researchers from participating in a symposium on brain trauma held in Havana. According to Marazul Charters, which had arranged the travel, OFAC asserted that "research cannot be done at a conference or in groups." Many scholars were quick to point out that dialogue is a crucial part of the process by which ideas are developed and tested. "OFAC just has a very narrow concept of research," said philosopher Kathy Russell of the State University of New York at Cortland.

E. Roy John, a professor at New York University's School of Medicine and director of the university's brain research laboratories, said that in areas like molecular biology and mathematics, Cuba was "world class." Stuart Youngner, a professor at Case Western Reserve University who helped organize the conference, called the OFAC action "an infringement on academic freedom [and] our freedom as citizens to travel." He added that the decision also damages science in the United States and around the world.

Other Effects of the Embargo

The tightened embargo affects more than just travel. OFAC notified professional journals this spring [2004] that editing articles by Cubans for publication was "providing a service to a Cuban national" and thus violates the embargo. In this new interpretation, "the reordering of paragraphs or sentences, correction of syntax [and] grammar, and replacement of inappropriate words by U.S. persons" is prohibited. Although the publication of Cuban articles is allowed, the editing of them is not, unless specifically licensed. So, presumably, Cuban articles can still be published, but they will have to have errors in spelling or grammar in them.

The embargo works both ways. It also prevents Cuban scholars and cultural figures from coming to the United States. The U.S. State Department has increasingly denied visas to Cubans who want to attend professional meetings or lecture at U.S. universities. Among the reasons given for the denials is that a professor is an employee of the Cuban government. Indiana State University political scientist Michael Erisman has pointed out that so, too, are "all those U.S. academics who work in public institutions." Last year, over 150 Cuban musicians and artists were similarly denied visas, including all potential award winners at the Latin Grammys. With those denials, the government infringed yet again on intellectual freedom, further isolating us behind the embargo wall.

The longest-standing academic exchange with Cuba is based at Johns Hopkins University. It began jointly with Yale and Columbia universities in 1977, during a thaw in U.S.-Cuban relations, when sixteen Cuban scholars were permitted to come to the United States. As it became increasingly difficult for Cubans to get visas from the State Department, the program became less an exchange and more a one-way relationship, with Hopkins students and faculty going to Cuba for an annual winter intersession course. "The U.S. government has been obstructionist," commented Hopkins history professor Franklin Knight before the advent of the new regulations. Now, under these new regulations, even this short course in Cuba is threatened. OFAC has informed Hopkins that after twenty-seven years, its license will not be automatically renewed.

Also effectively curtailed are the institutional licenses that increasing numbers of universities had obtained to authorize their faculty, students, and administrators to travel to Cuba for educational programs, research, and even teaching. The licenses gave great flexibility to educators and were especially useful in developing ongoing exchange programs with Cuban institutions.

The Cuba Obsession

In 2003, OFAC, which enforces sanctions against several countries, terrorist networks, and drug traffickers worldwide, spent $3.3 million of its $21.2 million budget on Cuba. Twenty-one of its 120 employees were assigned to work on the Cuba embargo. Yet OFAC had only four employees investigating Osama bin Laden's and Saddam Hussein's wealth. Since 1990, OFAC has opened just ninety-three enforcement investigations related to terrorism, but 10,683 investigations related to the

Cuba sanctions. Administrative hearings against the first of those accused of illegal travel to Cuba were to begin in July.

In addition, for nearly a year before the introduction of the new regulations, the U.S. Department of Homeland Security had been inspecting those boarding direct charter flights to Cuba, blocking many from their travel at the last minute. In the two months before January 2004, the department and OFAC interviewed more than 44,000 travelers to Cuba. Senator Max Baucus of Montana, who requested the OFAC statistics cited above, complained after receiving them that "rather than spending precious resources to prevent Americans from exercising their right to travel, OFAC must realign its priorities and instead work harder to keep very real terrorist threats out of our country and prevent another September 11."

Nevertheless, the Bush administration announced plans in May to sharply increase its spending on anti-Castro propaganda worldwide and within Cuba, while also fostering a political opposition in Cuba. Under the rubric of aiding "the training, development, and empowerment of a Cuban democratic opposition and civil society," $29 million will be added to the $7 million already allocated for such purposes. Would any self-respecting sovereign nation accept such blatant intervention in its internal political affairs? How would the United States respond if, say, China financed a political opposition here?

Not only has Congress turned against the embargo, but most Cuban Americans even now favor a constructive engagement with Cuba.

But interference in Cuba has long been a staple of U.S. policy. As a means to foster regime change, the embargo against Cuba has been supported by both Republicans and Democrats through nine administrations. Only in recent years has this relic of the Cold War come up against bipartisan opposition. Congress has voted in favor of easing the embargo for four years in a row. This year, both houses of Congress attached identical amendments to the appropriations bill for the Departments of Transportation and Treasury that would have stripped funding for enforcement of the travel restrictions. The amendment would have opened up travel to Cuba to everyone. Even though the amendment was passed by large majorities in both houses, it was unilaterally removed from the bill by the Republican leadership at the request of the White House.

Not only has Congress turned against the embargo, but most Cuban Americans even now favor a constructive engagement with Cuba. According to a new report from the Latin American Working Group titled *Ignored Majority: The Moderate Cuban-American Community*, 75 percent of Cuban Americans feel that the embargo has not worked. Sixty-eight percent believe that residents of Cuba should decide how and when the political system there should change. The mission of the Latin American Working Group is to encourage U.S. policies toward Latin America that promote human rights, justice, peace, and sustainable development.

> *Instead of changing Cuban minds, people-to-people contact was changing American minds.*

Not Just for Academics

In recent years, the largest number of legal U.S. visitors to Cuba (after Cuban Americans) went under the people-to-people educational licenses that allowed people from various walks of life to travel to Cuba on educational programs that emphasized direct contact with ordinary Cubans. Thousands of Americans went to Cuba this way. In the minds of some anti-Castro groups, the rationale for allowing this exception to the embargo was that Americans would bring their ideas and values to the Cuban people, thereby undermining popular support for Castro and socialism. This ideological approach supplemented the main track of U.S. policy, which sought to weaken the Cuban government by more aggressive means, an approach that many had come to recognize as a failure after four decades.

Many people believed that OFAC canceled people-to-people licenses in spring 2003 because, rather than eroding popular support for the Cuban government, travel to Cuba was giving Americans a positive impression of what the Cuban Revolution had accomplished and making them critical of U.S. policy. Instead of changing Cuban minds, people-to-people contact was changing American minds. So OFAC terminated the program, claiming that it was a form of disguised tourism that brought U.S. dollars to the Castro government. No longer would ordinary citizens be allowed to penetrate the iron curtain their government had built between them and the seductions of Cuban socialism.

Ending these nonacademic educational programs raises a fundamental question for the academic community. Is intellectual freedom just for academics? Scholars have long enjoyed a privileged exception to the embargo. Almost any professor could travel freely to Cuba for purposes of research without specific governmental approval. This policy was based on "the conviction that the unfettered search for knowledge is indispensable for the strengthening of a free and orderly world," as the AAUP's [American Association of University Professors] former general secretary Mary Burgan wrote in a March 2004 letter to OFAC protesting the barring of U.S. scholars from participating in the Cuban conference on brain trauma mentioned above. Doesn't this principle apply as well to ordinary citizens?

After people-to-people licenses were eliminated last year [2003], academics pursuing research accounted for the second largest category of travelers after families with relatives in

Cuba. With both of these two categories sharply curtailed, research by individual scholars may well be next to be cut entirely.

It is often not fully appreciated what a rich culture the embargo is walling us off from.

Isolating the United States

As Supreme Court Justice William O. Douglas wrote in 1964, "The right to know, to converse with others, to consult with them, to observe social, physical, political, and other phenomena abroad as well as at home gives meaning and substance to freedom of expression and freedom of the press."

It is often not fully appreciated what a rich culture the embargo is walling us off from. "Cuban scholarship has flourished under the revolution across the board," says Franklin Knight of Johns Hopkins. "We would not have known this if not for our exchange. Personally, I have benefited tremendously." Through the Hopkins exchange program, Knight has been active in archival work in Cuba, sending computers there and training librarians to digitize documents (it took three years to get U.S. approval to export twenty-six computers). "The new restrictions hurt us," says Knight. "Cuba is an integral part of the Americas and has been since 1492. Its archives are vital to understanding this."

Jualynne Dodson is another scholar who has built a career on research on Cuba. She does ethnographic field research on African religious traditions in Cuba, exploring the intricacies of popular religious culture. Formerly at the University of Colorado, she moved her African Atlantic research team to Michigan State University, where she is training a new cadre of young scholars to explore the incorporation of African-based culture into the character of Cuban national identity.

Cuba is well known for its vibrant music, cinema, and arts. It is also on the cutting edge of biotechnology research.

Researchers there carry out important archeological and environmental work; they have identified rare exotic species and cultivated a world-class orchid garden. Indeed, the social project of the revolution itself offers to the social sciences a unique experiment in transforming a neocolonial society. While Cuba's accomplishments are widely appreciated worldwide, the embargo isolates us in the United States from the island's cultural scene.

The meetings of the Latin American Studies Association have long provided a venue for scholarly exchanges with Cubans. More than seventy Cubans came to the association's 2000 meeting; they were one of the largest delegations from outside the United States. (Most were sponsored by the association, because the embargo denies Cuba access to the dollars needed to fund travel by scholars.) Only five Cubans, however, attended the association's 2003 meeting, because the State Department denied visas to most of the 103 Cuban scholars invited. Not many Cubans are expected at this fall's meeting for the same reason. Members of the association have suggested that meetings be held abroad so that scholars from throughout the Americas can participate free of U.S. governmental interference.

Philosophers and the Embargo Wall

The field of philosophy offers an example of what gets lost as a result of barring U.S. academics from contact with Cuba. For more than twenty years—from 1959 to 1982—there was virtually no contact between philosophers in the two countries. Then, during the [Jimmy] Carter administration, travel opened up briefly. In 1982, philosopher Edward D'Angelo, who was then at the University of Bridgeport, organized a small delegation to go to Havana for the first conference between U.S. and Cuban philosophers since the revolution. Cliff DuRand, co-author of this article, was one of the delegates. He remembers, "We flew on a chartered flight out of Newburg

International Airport in the middle of the night, direct to Havana. It was like going from one world to another distant land." That encounter involved only six U.S. philosophers, but as small as it was, it was the beginning of a bridge between philosophers from both sides of the wall that had long separated them. While the group was in Havana, the [Ronald] Reagan administration prohibited travel once again.

It wasn't until 1990 that the second such conference was held between U.S. and Cuban philosophers. After that, the conference occurred annually, involving as many as 90 delegates from the United States and 140 Cubans. In addition, it was broadened to include the social sciences as well as the humanities. It became the premier intellectual event in Havana as Cuban thinkers welcomed their neighbors to the north after the collapse of the Soviet Union and Eastern Europe, where most of them had received their graduate education. To date, the North American delegations, organized by DuRand, have brought seven hundred academics to Cuba. Many have returned again and again, developing collaborative relationships with their Cuban counterparts.

In spite of the blockade, it has been possible to build relationships across the wall, even though each U.S. administration has been hostile to Cuba. "It hasn't been easy. It has taken persistence. It has taken commitment. It has even taken political struggle," says DuRand. In 1998, OFAC denied licenses to DuRand's entire delegation less than a week before its scheduled departure. Delegates nationwide called their congressional representatives, who in turn bombarded OFAC with inquiries until it relented. On the day the delegates were supposed to leave, the licenses came through. Most made it to Havana in time for the opening of the conference. "Intellectual freedom isn't free," DuRand concludes. "It takes struggle to win it."

This past July, hundreds of people from all walks of life took up this struggle by testing OFAC's restrictions following the cancellation of people-to-people travel licenses. In an open, public travel challenge, the humanitarian group Pastors for Peace brought material aid to the people of Cuba. Fifty tons of medicines, computers, and school supplies collected from across the United States were taken to Cuba without a license. The group was joined by two other organizations, the Venceremos Brigade and the African Awareness Association, in a massive act of civil disobedience affirming the right to travel freely. After spending nine days in Cuba, the protesters broke through the wall once again by bringing into the United States forbidden Cuban goods, such as medicines not available here.

As famed abolitionist Frederick Douglass said in the nineteenth century, "Power concedes nothing without a demand. It never has and it never will."

3

The Embargo Should Not Be Lifted

Investor's Business Daily

Although many are calling for an end to sanctions against Cuba now that Raul Castro is in power, lifting the embargo too soon would only serve to further benefit the Castro regime. Lifting the embargo will do nothing to further the cause of democracy in the region. In fact, it would only provide Castro with additional power to control Cubans and increase feelings of aggression toward the United States.

Diplomacy: Now that Fidel Castro has resigned, calls for lifting the embargo on U.S. trade with Cuba grow louder. Bad idea. It not only forgets why the ban is there at all, but also fortifies the Castro family's grip on power.

Calling for an End to the Embargo

It didn't take long for the most naive of the Democratic presidential candidates, Barack Obama, a critic of the 1962 U.S. embargo, to call for its end.

"If the Cuban leadership begins opening Cuba to meaningful democratic change, the United States must be prepared to begin taking steps to normalize relations and ease the embargo of the last five decades," he said last week [February, 2008].

Sounds like a fresh start, but in reality, it's no different from existing U.S. policy toward Cuba. The U.S., which put the embargo in place and tightened it after Castro confiscated American properties, murdered U.S. citizens and tried to launch a nuclear attack against us, will indeed drop the embargo if democratic changes occur. That's the same as the candidate of "change."

So the nuance in Obama's statement comes from his repeated criticism of the embargo and in his emphasis on lifting it. "It's absolutely true that I think our policy has been a failure," he said Thursday.

His calls for democracy there are window-dressing, and a double standard to his stated opposition to approving vastly improved Colombia for a free trade pact. Worse, his record voting in the Senate against TV Marti [created by the U.S. government to provide news programming to Cuba] which would provide Cubans with real news, suggests he's insincere about promoting democracy, to say the least.

Embargo in place, the U.S. is still Cuba's largest food supplier, shipping $2 billion since 2001, $438 million last year alone.

More Critics of the Embargo

But he's not alone. Pundits and lobbyists have also stepped up calls to give the Castro brothers what they want and end the trade embargo now that [Fidel Castro's brother] Raul is running things and rumored to be a Chinese-style economic liberal. Like Obama, most package their calls as a democracy move in this context, with varying sincerity.

It's a smoke screen. There's nothing in the dynastic succession of Raul Castro to head Cuba's government—while his brother Fidel retains leadership of the Communist party—to suggest that Cuba will liberalize. Oh, there may be cosmetic changes—a handful of Cuba's 230 political prisoners might be released, but no solemn rights to read, organize, associate with or buy what one wants will happen. Those kinds of reforms would threaten the regime.

Castro Wants the Embargo Lifted

Calls to end the embargo are rooted in Castro's own propaganda. Cuba's oligarchs blame communism's failures on the embargo—not their own central planning, excessive control and waste of human talent.

In reality, the U.S. trade embargo has little to do with that, and is very mild. It lets U.S. food and medicine go to Cuba, freeing the Castro brothers of any need to create a viable economy. Cuba trades with every country in the world already, and many ship U.S. goods to Cuba indirectly. Still, it's a sump of poverty and backwardness.

Embargo in place, the U.S. is still Cuba's largest food supplier, shipping $2 billion since 2001, $438 million last year alone. Medical supplies totaled an estimated $20 million. Private aid was $270 million, and exiles sent $1 billion back last year.

Cuba Is Not Like China

But Cuba apologists call the embargo off-kilter because the U.S. trades with other communist regimes, like China and Vietnam.

True, but conditions aren't the same. Both China and Vietnam want to be friends and liberalized their regimes in 1976 and 1986, respectively, creating vast private sectors before any trade began. When a U.S. citizen buys a Made In China radio at Wal-Mart, he's strengthening China's private sector—and future democracy.

Cuba hasn't a scintilla of that in place. Its military (led by Raul Castro) controls all business in Cuba. There is no private sector at all.

Increased Suffering

In fact, penury [poverty] is the sole spur toward liberalization in Cuba.

When the Soviets cut off $3 billion in annual aid in 1991, the Castro brothers briefly let people operate restaurants and hostels from their houses. When Venezuela's petrotyrant began shipping Cuba $1 billion in de facto free oil, the restaurants were shut down.

Meanwhile, six days after two congressmen proposed a bill to lighten the embargo on March 12, 2003, Castro launched his hardest crackdown on dissidents in years, imprisoning 75. It's a pattern.

There's little doubt that Raul and his cronies would act the same way to new U.S. moves to open trade, because they control the entire economy. They wouldn't just line their own pockets; they'd use that power to end freedoms and step up their hostility to the U.S.

That's a problem we don't need. Unless Raul Castro permits hard freedoms, like a private sector, free information, democratic elections and an end to imprisoning those who speak out, ending the embargo will benefit only him. It's about time the naive proponents of what the Castro regime wants grasp this reality.

4

The U.S. Policy in Cuba Is Counterproductive

Wayne S. Smith

Wayne S. Smith is a former chief of the U.S. Interests Section in Havana and is currently a senior fellow at the Center for International Policy in Washington.

The U.S. Policy in Cuba will not succeed as long as threats against the Cuban government stand at the center of the strategy and human rights violations by the U.S. at Guantanamo Bay serve as the example of democracy in Cuba. Further, curtailing travel between the U.S. and Cuba does little to block revenue in Cuba but much to keep American ideals of democracy from entering into the landscape of ordinary Cubans. The U.S. must change its policy if it wants to effect positive change on the island.

The outcome of the election in Iraq [2005] is encouraging, to be sure. Elections for a national assembly, however, are only a beginning. And if the United States is to point Iraq and various other societies toward democracy, it must go back to the adage that "one leads best by setting an example."

Leading by Example

We have not been doing that. Not with the images coming out Abu Ghraib and other U.S. military prisons in Iraq, Afghanistan and Guantanamo Bay. And now we have reports that the

Wayne S. Smith, "Our Cuba Policy Will Get U.S. Nada," *The Atlanta Journal-Constitution*, February 2, 2005, p. A15. Copyright © The Atlanta Journal-Constitution. Republished with permission of The Atlanta Journal-Constitution, conveyed through Copyright Clearance Center, Inc.

interim Iraqi government appointed by the United States had also been torturing prisoners while U.S. officials looked the other way. Following our example? This is not the way to build a democracy.

And how ironic it is that Cuba, described by Condoleezza Rice in her confirmation hearings for secretary of state as "an outpost of tyranny," on Jan. 19 [2005] presented a formal protest to the U.S. government over the torture of prisoners at the Guantanamo Naval Base, which is in Cuba. And the reports of torture on which the Cubans base their protest come not from the so-called liberal press, but from FBI agents who were on the base, and from the International Red Cross.

Cuba is a case in point in other ways as well. The [George W.] Bush administration urges it to release political prisoners, provide fair trials and to respect other civil liberties. Fine. But then we see that the Bush administration itself has decided to construct a special facility at Guantanamo in which some 200 so-called "illegal enemy combatants" will be held indefinitely, with no resort whatever to anything resembling due process. The government simply considers them dangerous, on the basis of evidence it never intends to reveal. A tale right out of [Czech writer] Franz Kafka. What kind of example are we setting?

The Bush administration's approach is counterproductive.

U.S. Policy Failing

Most Americans want to see political prisoners released in Cuba and to see Cuba move toward a more open society. But that will not be brought about by U.S. threats and efforts to isolate. And now the Bush administration says its objective is to bring down the Cuban government.

Inevitably, the Cuban government has reacted to that by tightening its defenses and demanding even greater internal discipline. That is hardly surprising. It is what one would have expected. But it is the exact opposite of what we should want to see. In other words, the Bush administration's approach is counterproductive.

It is also doomed to failure. Restricting Cuban-Americans and other U.S. citizens from traveling reduces Cuban revenues somewhat, but there are still plenty of European tourists—and revenues. Moreover, there is a distinct downside to travel controls. It has always been an article of faith in the United States that the travel of American citizens abroad is the best way to spread the message of American democracy. Or as Elizardo Sanchez, Cuba's leading human rights activist, has often put it: "The more American citizens in the streets of Cuban cities, the better for the cause of a more open society. So why do you maintain travel controls?"

An excellent question.

U.S. policy discourages rather than encourages peaceful change.

Support for Dissidents

Another measure is to be increased U.S. support for the internal opposition, or "the dissidents." But here again, the result is likely to be minimal. The dissidents have a legitimate role to play in trying to expand the parameters for freedom of expression, assembly and other civil rights. They do not have anything like the strength or capability to pose any kind of threat to the government. Nor, as most of them see it, is that their role. Indeed, for the Bush administration to suggest that they are its instruments in trying to bring an end to their own government opens them to charges of being "foreign agents." It is irresponsible on the part of the administration to put them in that position.

In her confirmation hearings, Rice said the administration supports Oswaldo Paya, one of Cuba's leading dissidents. Well, perhaps. But I was in Cuba for several days just before the inauguration and had a long conversation with Paya, whom I have known for years. The administration's policy toward Cuba, he said, was not really helpful. He and his colleagues most of all want to bring about an internal dialogue and the liberation of their colleagues jailed in 2003, a few of whom have already been released. U.S. policy impedes rather than advances both causes.

Neither Paya nor his colleagues will accept material support from the United States and they have no thought of bringing down the government; rather, they want to bring about change through peaceful and legal means. U.S. policy, he said, simply makes that more difficult.

Paya is right. U.S. policy discourages rather than encourages peaceful change. At the same time, the Castro regime, thanks to a new oil field, a new economic relationship with China and sizable payments coming in from Venezuela for the services of the thousands of Cuban doctors there, is doing much better economically. It is in no danger whatever of collapse. The Bush approach, in short, leads nowhere.

5

Cuba Is Not a Threat to
the U.S.

Fred Reed

Fred Reed was previously a columnist for the Washington Times
and is currently a writer living near Guadalajara in Mexico.

*Cubans are suffering both because of Castro's regime and be-
cause of U.S. policy. The embargo against Cuba is used by Castro as an excuse for further oppressing the Cuban people, who
live with immense economic challenges and little freedom. Although the U.S. claims that Cuba is a threat, Cuba has no real
military. Further, the U.S. has almost no international support
and waning internal support for its policy against Cuba. It is
time for the U.S. to change its policy toward Cuba and help ease
the poverty for the people who reside there.*

On Havana's Malecon, the seawall that parallels the shore,
the waves roll in and hit the sudden obstacle, sending
towering explosions of bright white spray far into the air, oc-
casionally soaking the unwary pedestrian. Across the highway
that follows the malecon is a cheap open-air restaurant, the
DiMar. A steady breeze from the sea pours across the tables. A
tolerable shrimp cocktail, topped with mayonnaise, costs a few
bucks. On a couple of evenings, I drank a beer there, watching
Cuba go by. It wasn't what I had expected.

Unlike many gringo tourists, I was legal, having gotten a
license from the Treasury Department. Without one, travel to

5
5

Cuba is illegal under the Trading with the Enemy Act of 1917. Why Cuba was my enemy wasn't clear to me. Nor was it to the Cubans.

The country is poor, run down, and itself almost a museum.

I had inadvertently neglected to tell the authorities that I was a journalist—I hate it when that happens—so I was not in a position to ask probing questions of officials. But then I didn't want official twaddle. I wanted to wander, take cabs down the coast, just look at things. And I did.

Life in Havana

I was pleased to find the old part of Havana both charming and reasonably well preserved, especially around the Convent of San Francisco. It is, of course, a museum now, as God knows we mustn't be religious, but it is in good shape and breathes a moody solemnity. I tried to imagine the stillness in times before the motorcycle. The narrow lanes around it were closed to cars, making it pleasant to walk among the shops.

The country is poor, run down, and itself almost a museum. Sitting in the DiMar is like visiting the Fifties. The American embargo makes it hard to get new cars, so many Cubans still drive models from 1959, the year of the revolution, and before. Some sport jazzy paint jobs, and others don't. It was remarkable to watch the rides of my adolescence go by, charting them mentally as one did in 1964—'54 Merc, '57 Caddy, '56 Chevy. Around me the other customers, downscale Cubans in all shades of nonwhite, laughed and chatted.

They are an accommodating people. On my arrival, they spoke a truncated Spanish hard to understand—*Como etah uteh? Ma o menoh*—but they made an intense national effort to improve their clarity, and by my fourth day, they were comprehensible.

Cuba doesn't fit its sordid image. It is most assuredly a dictatorship, yet the police presence is much less than that of Washington, and such cops as I saw had no interest in me. It is not regimented. Havana does not feel oppressed, as Moscow did during the days of the Soviet Union. Mao's China it isn't.

Cuba Is Not a Threat

The island certainly isn't dangerous to anyone. Somebody said that the only communists remaining in the world are in Cuba, North Korea, and the Harvard faculty lounge. I do not know whether Harvard's professoriate thirsts for godless world hegemony, though the idea is not implausible, but it is absurd to put North Korea and Cuba in the same category. Pyongyang [capital of North Korea] has, or wants, nuclear arms, and has both a huge army aimed at South Korea and a habit of testing long-range ballistic missiles. Cuba has little military and no one to use it against; from an American point of view, the Cuban armed forces are about as terrifying as George Will with a water pistol. It has no nuclear arms and no signs of wanting any. It is not a rogue state. It is a bedraggled island of pleasant people who need money.

I do not think that communism generates poverty; rather it finds it and preserves it.

Cuba is expensive. Figuring the prices of things is difficult—deliberately so, one might suspect—because of a peculiar game that the government plays with currencies. Cuba has two, the national currency, which a visitor almost never sees, and the CUC (pronounced "kook"), which appears to exist to impoverish tourists. If you change dollars, the government skims 20 percent off the top and then changes the rest at $1.08 per CUC. If you change Mexican pesos, which I did, the rate is 13.3 pesos per CUC when the dollar was trading at about 11 pesos. Visitors have to buy things for CUC's, which the seller then has to exchange for national currency at a rate of . . . You see, nobody seems sure what anything really costs.

The island could use some investment. While I found neighborhoods with nice looking modern houses, said by taxi drivers to belong to governmental officials and employees of foreign firms, the rest of Havana needs paint, repairs, and new sidewalks. Countless once elegant houses with pillared porches and tall windows are now discolored and crumbling.

Communism in Cuba

Why communists imagine themselves to be revolutionary is a mystery. Whenever they gain power in a country, it comes to a dead stop and sits there as other countries pass it by. I do not think that communism generates poverty; rather it finds it and preserves it. It has certainly done so here. Cuba seems firmly mired in 1959. How much of this comes from the embargo—el bloqueo as the Cubans call it—and how much from communism, I don't know. Nobody does. This is convenient for [Fidel] Castro, as he can blame everything on the United States, which he does.

Washington has become Fidel and his brother Raul's irreplaceable supporter. On roadsides, along Havana's malecon, in little Mediterranean-looking villages down the coast, one sees signs of the type, "43 hours of the blockade would pay for a new school house"—or buy so many locomotives or complete the national highway or this or that. How the figures are arrived at, I don't know, but it doesn't matter. To an extent, the signs are not propaganda, but simply call attention to a fact: the embargo does hurt people who want jobs, dollars from tourists, and consumer goods. They are perfectly aware why they don't have them—the American embargo. This may or may not always be quite true, but it has a convincing verisimilitude. It makes Fidel look good. He is standing up to the bastards who are strangling us.

How resolutely communist are the Cuban people? This is just an impression, but I would say not at all, if that much. Abstractions ending in "-ism" are hobbies for people who have time for them. Everyone I talked to wanted more money—a better job, better food, better clothes, a chance to take the wife out to dinner. After these, more freedom.

The Embargo Is an Excuse

As an example of Castro's use of the embargo to maintain himself in power, consider the Internet. People I talked to had heard of it, of course, but had little idea what it was and no access to it. It can be found in hotels and apparently in tourist areas, though I didn't see a single cybercafe of the sort that are found every 20 feet in all Third World countries I know. Why no Internet? Cubans universally said that the U.S. embargo prevented Cuba from having access. This struck me as improbable. It was.

Washington in effect aids Castro in maintaining censorship.

At ZDNet, a respectable American website dealing with matters electronic, I later found an account of a UN conference in Athens in which a Cuban official was asked what percentage of Cubans have access to the Net. He dodged the question frantically. ZDNet quotes Bill Woodcock, a network engineer and research director of Packet Clearing House, as follows: "Zero percent of Cubans are connected to the Internet. The Cuban government operates an incumbent phone company, which maintains a Web cache. Cubans who wish to use the Internet browse the government Web cache. They do not have unrestricted access to the Internet." And if they did, the government would find itself with a lot of explaining to do.

Also from ZDNet: "A report published last month by the Reporters Without Borders advocacy group says, 'It is forbidden to buy any computer equipment without express permission from the authorities,' and spyware 'installed in all Internet cafes automatically detects banned content.' U.S. law exempts telecommunications equipment and service from the trade embargo."

The Cuban government isn't lying after all—who would have thought it? It actually can blame lack of access on the embargo. Washington in effect aids Castro in maintaining censorship.

The Cuban Economy

Cuba has what are called "coco-taxis"—yellow spherical plastic things like part of a coconut husk attached to a motorcycle, providing transportation for two. Having hired a coco-taxi for a day, I got to know the driver reasonably well, to the point of being invited to his house for snacks. His wife had just had a new daughter, and he was to no end proud of both. His take on the economy was that things were bad, had been worse, but were slowly getting better. Still, he said, taxes were high, and he had to buy gasoline in CUC's, which made it more expensive. Things like computers were out of reach, and he and his wife couldn't afford restaurants. Did he have many gringo fares, I asked. No, not many. He wished more would come. He was tired of being poor.

I am not sure why it is in the national interest of the United States to make a cabdriver and his family live on rice and fish. I did not feel notably safer on hearing about it.

The Embargo Is Not Effective

An embargo makes sense when it makes sense, but doesn't when it doesn't. Cuba is no longer the spearhead of the Soviet Union. Indeed, according to many observers, there is no Soviet Union. We seem to proceed from pure vengefulness against Castro. Fidel, a freelance reprehensible dictator, beat Battista [the regime that ruled Cuba prior to Castro], our reprehensible dictator. We want to get even.

But Castro is not Cuba. The CIA World Factbook says that Cuba has 11,394,043 citizens. One of them is Castro, and 11,394,042 are not. Many Americans say that Castro is evil, and so we need to embargo him. But one person the embargo assuredly does not hurt is Castro. Does anyone think he eats less well because of it?

Cuban Americans

Ah, but there are the Cuban emigres in Miami. So much of American foreign policy seems determined by domestic politics, by a certain infantile truculence, and by ignorance of how people work. The embargo has accomplished nothing of any use for 50 years. Clearly the thing to do is keep at it for another 50. The "Cubans" in Miami demand it.

We are subject to considerable disinformation regarding the island. The Cuban emigres in south Florida paint Cuba as a hellhole. It isn't. I've seen hellholes. Even before coming to Cuba, I had developed a dim view of the pseudo-Cubans of Miami. They were arrogant, and rude to Anglos if not actually hostile. I found myself wanting to ask, "Just whose country do you think this is anyway?" But the answer was obvious.

By supporting the embargo, they are knowingly inflicting grave hardship on 11 million of their supposed fellows because they are mad at Fidel. This is contemptible. They want the U.S. to get back for them holdings that Castro confiscated on coming to power. Given the corruption and criminality rampant under Battista, it would be interesting to ask just how they came by their property. To try to get it back, they are perfectly willing to condemn the island's population to another 50 years of living on fish and rice. What patriots.

It is worth noting that 1959 was 48 years ago. The great majority of these alleged Cubans were born in the U.S., have never been to Cuba, and wouldn't live there if they could. They are gringos, Americans. They are also an important voting bloc in a state crucial to any presidential candidate. As is so often the case in foreign policy, domestic politics trump national interest and coherent thought.

Cuba: Another Perspective

Living as I do in Mexico, perhaps I have a better angle of view on matters Latin-American than do ideological isolates in Washington. To the world below Laredo [Texas], Cuba is a heroic little country being bullied by the U.S., but not giving in. I'm not sure this isn't the opinion of the whole world except for America. Remember that much of Latindom believes that South America's economic doldrums spring from American exploitation. They don't: considerable faith is required to believe that Bolivia would turn into Japan if only the U.S. stopped oppressing it. But beliefs, not facts, determine behavior.

American arguments against the island don't carry much weight in a region that sees things through Latin American eyes. For example, by regional standards Cuba isn't terribly poor. It didn't suffer the butchery of Guatemala and El Salvador. For 50 years it has been politically stable. Given the experience of Latin Americans with dictatorship, corruption, and violence, Cuba's government doesn't look bad.

The problem is not Castro. It is the hostility of Washington.

Americans, perhaps because of the Cold War, tend to think that communism is communism, all poured from the same bucket. Not so. At the high end of horror, you have [Joseph] Stalin, [Prime Minister of Cambodia] Pol Pot, and Mao, genuine madmen of genocidal enthusiasms. North Korea's dynasty runs a close second.

Castro is neither mad nor genocidal. A dictator, yes. A tiresome windbag, yes. Repressive of dissent, yes—but willingness to repress dissent doesn't mean that there is a great deal of dissent to repress. As far as Cubans are concerned—I mean real Cubans, the kind who live in Cuba, not the make-believe variety in Miami—the problem is not Castro. It is the hostility of Washington. Castro could end the embargo by surrendering, sure. Washington could end it by ending it, and probably end Castro at the same time.

While I was on the island, the UN voted 184 to 4 to recommend that the United States end the embargo. In this vote, America had the support of the following great powers: Israel, Palau, and the Marshall Islands. Several Cubans spontaneously told me of the vote, smiling triumphantly. Intrigued, I made a point of bringing the vote up with people I ran into. They all knew of it—the governmental television made very sure of it—and grinned broadly over what they saw as a victory for Cuba over Bush.

If this island is unstable, yearning for Fidel to die so that it can revolt and become an appendage of the U.S., I'm Sophia of Anhalt-Zerbst.

A View of Havana

I spent several hours walking through Havana's slums. These are extensive and ugly. Like so much of the city, they seem to have been built 50 years ago and never maintained. Commercial streets have the usual pillars, often in pastel colors now covered with soot, the plaster falling off in patches. In side streets, potholes gape. Sometimes water, probably sewage, runs across the pavement. I saw nothing suggesting hunger, no potbellied malnutrition, but these people clearly have little. Time and again, I glanced into doorways and saw cruddy worn steps rising into darkness. Tired people gazed from windows.

Similar places exist in downtown Detroit and in Washington D.C., where abandoned buildings are common, where whole housing projects have their windows bricked up to keep them from becoming shooting galleries for needle people. In America, slums are racial in demarcation, but in Cuba they aren't. I encountered no hostility. In four hours, I didn't get so much as a hard look. In Detroit, I would have lasted five minutes. But these people are going nowhere—living, breeding, and dying with nothing to show for it. It is a rotten thing to do to them without very good reason. And there is no reason. It does not get rid of Fidel.

The trappings of bumper-sticker socialism are everywhere in Cuba. Signs on walls say "*¡Venceremos!*" ("We will conquer!") and "*¡Patria o Muerte!*" (Fatherland or death!) and other exciting things. Adolescence dies hard everywhere. A billboard shows pictures of [George W.] Bush, [Adolf] Hitler, and someone who perhaps was meant to be [Dick] Cheney (it looked like but can't have been John Lennon) with arithmetic notation: Bush plus whomever equals Hitler. Che Guevara's [Marxist revolutionary] face appears endlessly, the communist Christ, shot from slightly below, staring bravely off into a socialist paradise that didn't fit on the t-shirt. I saw postcard racks offering 13 different photos of Che. If he had severe acne scars and funny ears, he would be of no socialist importance, but he does make a good t-shirt.

The entire world—except Israel, the Marshall Islands, and Palau—is against the U.S. on this one.

Cuban Media

The press is assuredly controlled. The political section of a bookstore I saw consisted of maybe a dozen books about (sigh) Che, the rest being not much better. Confusingly, there were a couple of textbooks on business management. Television is heavy on affirmation of socialist patriotism. In particular, there are channels from China, which Cuba seems to regard as communist (when did you last hear of a communist economy growing at 10 percent, or at all?) and from Venezuela. Hugo Chavez clearly is thought to be a great man.

Toward the end of the adventure, I went back to the Di-Mar to commune with the wind and the exploding waves and ponder what I had seen. Cubans make good beer (Bucanero). I have to give them that, and while mayonnaise on shrimp may not seem advisable, it worked.

I wanted to sort out what I knew about Cuba from what I suspected, so as to avoid the trap of instant-expertism. Some things I did know. A hellhole? No. Threat to anyone? No. Danger to international stability? No. In need of embargoing? No. Dictatorship? Yes. Adherent of the Bill of Rights? No.

How bad was Fidel? I really didn't know. Admirers and detractors are wildly ideological. Compared to Thomas Jefferson, he doesn't look good, though I don't think Castro owns slaves. Compared to other dictators the U.S. has installed or supported—Somoza [an influential political family in Nicaragua], [Raphael] Trujillo, the Shah [leader of Iran], [Augusto] Pinochet, Saddam Hussein, and so on—about par.

But however repugnant Castro may be, the practical question is whether the embargo is in America's interest. If the United States is still strong enough that it doesn't have to care what the world thinks, then the embargo, though unnecessary, doesn't matter (except in moral terms, which don't matter). But as the country wages war on the Muslim world, tries to contain China (that's going to work), pushes Russia into China's arms, and tries to intimidate South America—all of these at once—maybe it would be better to improve America's relations with this hemisphere.

An effective way to spread communism is to make heroes of communists. The entire world—except Israel, the Marshall Islands, and Palau—is against the U.S. on this one. Is it so important to keep Miami happy?

6

Fidel Castro Ensured the Passage of the Helms-Burton Act

Edward J. González

Edward J. González is a first-generation Cuban American.

The United States needs to take a hard look at the goals and re-sults of the Helms-Burton Act (legislation that was enacted in 1996 to further impose sanctions on Cuba) and other policies aimed at Cuba. Not only has the Helms-Burton Act not been successful in bringing about the stated goals of the United States, it has furthered the atrocities of Fidel Castro's regime. In fact, Castro ensured the Act's passage by ordering two U.S. planes to be shot down shortly before the Act was to be voted on in Con-gress at a time when the U.S. was leaning toward easing restric-tions against Cuba. Since the Act's passage, the people of Cuba have endured additional hardships and no progress has been made toward removing the Castro regime from power.

What has come to be known unofficially as the Helms-Burton Act is legislation that was enacted by the US Congress in 1996 as H.R. 927, titled the *Cuban Liberty and Democratic Solidarity (LIBERTAD) Act of 1996.* The purpose of the act, in essence, was to further impose sanctions against Cuba, as a result of events current at that time, as well as to strengthen the sanctions already in place. In addition to numerous United Nations resolutions, as well as various international treaties, the Helms-Burton Act sought to further enforce requirements delineated by such US laws as the Cuban Democracy Act of 1992, the Foreign Assistance Act of 1961, and an amendment to this 1961 law, titled the Freedom Support Act.

Restrictions Nearly Lifted

In the weeks just prior to the dramatic birth of the Helms-Burton Act, Congress was debating *lifting* restrictions against Cuba, as a humanitarian gesture, as the fragile economic health of Cuba, following almost five years without support from the Soviet Union, became more apparent the act itself acknowledges this precipitous economic decline, in the opening statement of Section 2 (Section 1 being the Table of Contents), titled "FINDINGS." This section reads in part as follows, as taken from the Library of Congress Web site:

"The Congress makes the following findings:

1. The economy of Cuba has experienced a decline of at least 60 percent in the last 5 years as a result of—

2. (A) the end of its subsidization by the former Soviet Union of between 5 billion and 6 billion dollars annually;

   (B) 36 years of communist tyranny and economic mismanagement by the [Fidel] Castro government;

   (C) the extreme decline in trade between Cuba and the countries of the former Soviet bloc; and

   (D) the stated policy of the Russian Government and the countries of the former Soviet bloc to conduct economic relations with Cuba on strictly commercial terms.

3. At the same time, the welfare and health of the Cuban people have substantially deteriorated as a result of this

economic decline and the refusal of the Castro regime to permit free and fair democratic elections in Cuba.

4. The Castro regime has made it abundantly clear that it will not engage in any substantive political reforms that would lead to democracy, a market economy, or an economic recovery." ...

Fidel Castro must have taken notice and must have been concerned, for a softening of sanctions would impact his regime in a way counter to his plans and desires.

Fidel Castro Reacts

Through this act, from its opening lines, the Congress of the United States declared that the economy of Cuba at that time was in shambles, that the Cuban people were suffering as a result of it, and that Fidel Castro was not only the cause of these hardships, but was also entrenched in a manner that would assure the continued suffering of the people of Cuba. Taken out of context with the events of those days, the history of the contentious relationship between the US and Cuba, and the attitude toward Cuba in general at that time, it would appear that this opening volley could just as well have been made as part of a persuasive argument for the lifting of sanctions, the easing of the "substantially deteriorated" welfare and health of the Cuban people. This had appeared to be the direction that the Congress was headed in the weeks just prior to the introduction of this bill. But the easing of sanctions was discussed in Congress, and dutifully reported through the media, Fidel Castro must have taken notice and must have been concerned, for a softening of sanctions would impact his regime in a way counter to his plans and desires. Therefore, as was reported at the time, he instructed the Cuban Air Force to shoot down an unarmed surveillance plane over international waters. The plane was carrying Americans, was an aircraft licensed and registered in the US, and flown as part of a humanitarian mission by a group known as Brothers to the Rescue. The group is comprised mostly of Cuban exiles, and patrols the waters of the Florida straits looking for fleeing Cuban refugees on makeshift rafts. These rafts may carry them to freedom or just as easily to their deaths, as indicated by the number of empty rafts found, and documented in stories of survivors whose raft-mates failed to hang on in rough seas, who drowned and became fodder for sharks.

The Cuban people, in fear of the US, rallied around their nationalistic sentiments, fearing an invasion of Cuba, and endured further hardships, suffering, and misery.

The United States Responds

Naturally, the uproar caused by the downing of this private aircraft, along with the loss of lives was heard all the way to Congress, which, in typical, reactive fashion introduces, passed, and finally approved the Helms-Burton Act (LIBERTAD), H.R. 927, in record time. Quickly forgotten were the speeches and proclamations of the previous weeks in which the misery and suffering of the Cuban people was being upheld as a reason why the American embargo needed to be dismantled, or, at a minimum, readjusted in some form. Now Congress was laser-focused on punishing Castro for his flagrant disregard of international law and the sanctity of human lives.

In the immediate aftermath, as well as the months and years to come following the passage of the Helms-Burton Act, it has been evident that Congress played into Castro's manipulative tactics. Castro was able to further solidify his position through more of his fiery rhetoric, rallying crowds of Cubans into a nationalistic frenzy, citing the Helms-Burton Act as further proof of the imperialist, interventionist attitudes and desires of the US. Castro sold to the Cuban people that the one and only item on the US agenda for Cuba was complete and total domination. He further named the coming years *La Época Especial* (The Special Times), a time calling for further sacrifices from the Cuban people. Castro called for Cubans to stand vigilant against a forthcoming invasion by the United States, an invasion that would not liberate them from their hardships, but would instead enslave them to the United States.

This was no more and no less than the typical pack of lies that Castro had been serving us for thirty-six years, and that continue today. It served Castro well: The Cuban people, in fear of the US, rallied around their nationalistic sentiments, fearing an invasion of Cuba, and endured further hardships, suffering, and misery. As a direct result of the deft manipulation of Congress by a despot seeking nothing more than the continued iron-fisted rule of Cuba, and enabling himself and his inner circle to profit and live a life of luxury, Castro's subjects wallow in hopeless turmoil, essentially abandoned and incarcerated, with little to no resources, other than an incredible will to live and an attitude of *hay que resolver* (we have to resolve, we have to make do).

The Failure of Helms-Burton

Section 3 of the act, titled "PURPOSES," does not mention fostering fervent Cuban nationalism as a goal, but instead reads in its entirety:

"The purposes of this Act are—

1. to assist the Cuban people in regaining their freedom and prosperity, as well as in joining the community of democratic countries that are flourishing in the Western Hemisphere;

2. to strengthen international sanctions against the Castro government;

3. to provide for the continued national security of the United States in the face of continuing threats from the

Castro government of terrorism, theft of property from United States nationals by the Castro government, and the political manipulation by the Castro government of the desire of Cubans to escape that results in mass migration to the United States;

4. to encourage the holding of free and fair democratic elections in Cuba, conducted under the supervision of internationally recognized observers;

5. to provide a policy framework for United States support to the Cuban people in response to the formation of a transition government or a democratically elected government in Cuba; and

6. to protect United States nationals against confiscatory takings and the wrongful trafficking in property confiscated by the Castro regime."

In ten years from the inception of the Helms-Burton Act till now, it does not appear that there has been much success in achieving these declared goals.

The people of Cuba are much worse off today than they have ever been.

Item 1 of section 3 declares the honorable intent of the US government "to assist the Cuban people" to become, essentially, a free and prosperous society, productive members of the Caribbean community. The further strengthening of sanctions does not appear to have fostered the desired prosperity of Cuba, nor has it provided a vehicle through which to gain political freedoms necessary to achieve a democratic society. As proposed throughout this book, what it has done is further entrench Fidel Castro and his control over Cuba. The people of Cuba are much worse off today than they have ever been, yet there is no other future on the horizon for them because the embargo does not foster the dynamic undercurrents that need to occur in order for change to happen. Instead, it stifles them, slowly asphyxiating the Cuban people in an attempt to bring down Castro.

The terrorist plotting by Castro appears to be limited to blackmailing the United States as he can, with the threat of unleashing another flood of refugees at a moment's notice.

The Embargo Has No International Support

The second Item declares to rally the international community behind the American embargo as a means to dethrone Castro. This is where there is much debate within the exiled community. Many of the exiled Cubans I have spoken with will privately admit that the embargo is a failure, simply for the lack of support that the international community has provided for it. The major trading partners of the United States, some that are significant allies—such as England, Canada, Mexico, and the rest of the European Union—all conduct a brisk trade with Cuba, in clear, flagrant disregard of the embargo. These actions necessitate the suspension of Title III of the Act by the US president every six months. No matter which party has occupied the White House or controlled Congress, neither has been able to rally the international support needed to effectively enforce the provisions of the embargo. What if the United States rallied the international community behind this embargo, much like the recent economic embargo of Haiti, or the successful total embargo of the apartheid South African government throughout the eighties. That embargo culminated with the establishment of a democracy, with fair elections open to all races. That was an embargo that the great majority of the international community supported and strived to enforce, adjusting sanctions as needed, in order to deny the apartheid government the benefits of any loopholes it sought to exploit. The most significant factor that led to the successful implementation of this embargo against an entrenched government was the totality with which all nations joined it, evident in numerous resolutions issued by the United Nations. This is the exact ingredient lacking in the American embargo of Cuba.

Cuba Is Not a Threat to the United States

The third item declares how the United States is concerned about its properties in Cuba, the effect of terrorist plotting by Cuba toward the United States, and the manipulation by Fidel Castro of the Cuban people, where, at his whim, he can control a floodgate of refugees that can in a matter of days, if not hours, flood the shores of the United States, creating a disaster upon the affected Gulf states, notably Florida, overwhelming the capacity of local, state and federal agencies to effectively manage the onslaught. Many lives are placed at stake in these poker games, such as those lost during the last mass exodus, the Mariel boatlift of the summer of 1980. This is a legitimate concern for the United States, but it also speaks of the crises in Cuba, the hardships, misery, and lack of hope, wealth or health within her shores.

The terrorist plotting by Castro appears to be limited to blackmailing the United States as he can, with the threat of unleashing another flood of refugees at a moment's notice. In the weeks prior to the commencement of saber rattling toward Iraq by the George W. Bush administration, the administration floated a trial balloon declaring that Castro had biological weapons with the possible intent of terrorizing the United States. It was a fleeting item in the national media, laughable, showing the lengths to which the administration will go to appear to be doing something in the "War on Terror." Never mind effectively finishing the campaign in Afghanistan. Never mind the hijackers of September 11 who came from our "ally," Saudi Arabia, prior home of Osama bin Laden. Never mind focusing on the capture of our public enemy number one. Instead the administration felt compelled to increase the breadth and depth of its campaign against terror by suggesting that Cuba posed a serious threat to the United States. This proposal apparently died a quick death, leading to the selection of Iraq for further action in the "War on Terror," despite faulty "intelligence." This intelligence now seems to have been made up as the administration needed it, rather than based on facts and findings on the ground. In a way, I lament that the Bush administration did not pursue the premise of Cuba poised to attack the United States at any moment with weapons of biological terror. Perhaps this pursuit would at least have led to the removal of Fidel Castro, much like Saddam Hussein was ousted. In invading Cuba, the infighting would have been but a fraction of what has occurred in Iraq, and the loss of American lives would have been negligible, if any, much like the events that occurred when President [Ronald] Reagan ordered the US military to invade Grenada.

Other Goals of Helms-Burton

The Helms-Burton Act enumerates various military actions by the United States, as well as other sanctions brought against rogue nations with success. In particular it mentions the actions against Haiti, highlighting that these were sought through and sanctioned by the United Nations, which the United States has been unsuccessful in doing against Cuba.

The goal to encourage free and fair elections under international observers, as stated in item four of this third section, is a goal that deserves success. But again, without the international community's support of an embargo, this will not occur, as evident by the continued passage of years with no signs of valid, free and fair elections being held in Cuba.

Item five is probably of concern within the Cuban population, for it reeks of past interventionist activity by the United States. That the transitional government in Iraq was beset with problems from day one does not help. But more so, the history of the United States toward Cuba, as enshrined in the now-defunct Platt Amendment [an amendment appended to the Army Appropriations Act, passed in 1901, stipulating conditions for a US withdrawal from Cuba, following the Spanish-American war] is something that the Castro regime labors continuously and efficiently to keep in the forefront of the Cuban psyche, ready to be recalled whenever the words "United States" and "transitional government" are strung together.

What good would monetary compensation be when our families, friends, and compatriots continue to suffer?

Justice for Exiled Cubans

The last item is perhaps the most political, as it intends to appease the exiled Cuban population, residing within the United States, in particular those who have become naturalized citizens of this country. It seeks to provide these Cubans in particular, as well as other Americans who have had their assets and properties expropriated by Castro, with recourse to obtain compensation for their losses. My family, which had lived in Cuba for many generations, proud of our heritage, lost a lot of assets—property, homes, and other material items—to Castro, and the pain and suffering of these losses was coupled with the loss of our country. But what can we hope to gain through a law like this? The adage that "you can't squeeze blood out of a turnip" comes to mind. In addition, what good would monetary compensation be when our families, friends, and compatriots continue to suffer? How do you put a price tag on that? Rather than seeking financial compensation now through the courts of a foreign country, we should be seeking the return of democracy to Cuba, and then seek redress through her courts, on her terms, with a true jury of our peers. This portion of the Helms-Burton Act has further divided the Cuban communities. Those left to suffer in Cuba state that they have been left to *comerse el cable*—eat the wire. Those left behind have had to endure the hardships of a bleak daily life under the oppressive manipulations of Castro, while the rest of us in exile within the United States have been blessed with a life of relative luxury and comfort. This portion of the act has been interpreted among those in Cuba to mean that exiled Cubans are plotting to return to take what little is left. For the exiled community this has also fostered a split, in which those who had assets in Cuba are seen as wanting to return to a life pre-Castro, without paying any dues, by those who had to come to the United States or to other countries in order to build some, if any, measure of wealth. It can be seen as the classic crevasse between blue-collar and white-collared communities.

Apparently the humanitarian generosity which this great nation has shown in the past does not seem to apply to Cuba.

Blaming the United States

Other portions of the Helms-Burton Act bear discussion. Here are items 27 and 28 of section 2, the "FINDINGS" section.

(27) The Cuban people deserve to be assisted in a decisive manner to end the tyranny that has oppressed them for 36 years, and the continued failure to do so constitutes ethically improper conduct by the international community.

Given the date these words were written, we need to update "36 years" to "47 years." Item 27 again attempts to address the international community, this time by trying to shame them into action. But from a Cuban point of view this includes the United States, and the stigma of engaging in "ethically improper conduct" must be applied to the American government, as well. To continue a policy that the Helms-Burton Act admits has failed to remove Castro for 36 years is unethical and improper. The American embargo expired many years ago when the Kennedy administration dealt a murderous blow to the brave souls launched upon Bay of Pigs in 1961, and while secretly negotiating with Cuba and the Soviet Union during the missile crisis in October 1962. At that point a message was sent to the world that, in one way or another, the United States would compromise its principles, even if it meant the removal of its own backbone, causing the death of many men, as long as the agenda included items favorable to the interests of the United States, the Cuban exiles be damned if their interests didn't happen to fall within those parameters. And yet we wonder why the world does not support the embargo.

U.S. Interests in Cuba

At the time of the writing of the Helms-Burton Act, Fidel Castro had maintained his excruciating control over Cuba for 36 years. In the 28th item of section 2, the act declares that the national security interests of the United States had been at risk during that time due to Castro's regime. Yet item 1 of this same section states that the Cuban economy is on the brink of collapse, having declined at least 60 percent over five years. How can it be that a country with such an anemic, faltering economy, with a laughable military, and no longer receiving any support, economic or military, from the former Soviet Union, could pose a threat to the United States? The United States just flexing its military pinky could wipe the slate clean in Cuba. It was done in Grenada, Haiti, Iraq, and countless other military endeavors. Could the issue be a lack of courage? A hidden agenda, as some of the exiled leadership has alluded to? What purpose does it serve the United States, with a record of military responses toward countries that fail to appease it, to portray itself as intimidated by Fidel Castro? Granted, there are no vast reserves of oil under Cuban soil or waters, and its mineral resources are slight, so there is no economic incentive for the United States to have a democratic Cuba at its back door. Apparently the humanitarian generosity which this great nation has shown in the past does not seem apply to Cuba, save for those already here as exiles or naturalized citizens, the few lucky enough to touch U.S. soil and escape Fidel Castro's nightmare.

The Helms-Burton Act does include many provisions that are just and fair, or at a minimum, well-intentioned toward Cuba and her citizens.

Under section 306 of Title III of the Helms-Burton Act, the president of the United States can effectively suspend the initiation of portions of the act that directly seek remedy by United States nationals against the Cuban government for the loss of property. The president, upon proper notice to Congress, can suspend these portions of the act for six months at a time. During the time that the suspension is in effect, aggrieved individuals or entities cannot bring suit against Castro's regime. Since the passage and signing of the act in 1996, every president has suspended these portions of the act. The act further allows Cuban exiles and U.S. citizens to recover properties from people and entities from any country, that have been allowed by Fidel Castro to develop, maintain, and use them, as indicated under Title IV of the act. But since this includes all of the major trading partners of the United States, the president is placed in the position of either suspending those portions of the act, or essentially isolating the US from its trading partners, as these partners would be denied entry into the country, and their assets frozen and subject to confiscation as a means of providing remedy to individuals and entities seeking justice under provisions of the act.

Other Attempts of the Helms-Burton Act

The Helms-Burton Act does include many provisions that are just and fair, or at a minimum, well-intentioned toward Cuba and her citizens. It provides for the continued support of television and radio transmission to Cuba in an effort to provide Cubans with a truthful counterpoint to views emanating from Castro. Unfortunately, the current administration of George W. Bush has cut funding for these programs, and is quietly seeking to eliminate them altogether.

The act provides for a road map delineating how a transitional government could move into place and then assist the election of a permanent government. The drawbacks of this have been mentioned above.

The act details the aforementioned attacks on three private aircrafts by two Cuban Air Force jets, over international waters in 1996. That section within the Act, section 116, further provides evidence of the continued human rights abuses by Castro and his regime, and concludes with the following three items:

(b) STATEMENTS BY THE CONGRESS- (1) The Congress strongly condemns the act of terrorism by the Castro regime in shooting down the Brothers to the Rescue aircraft on February 24, 1996.

(2) The Congress extends its condolences to the families of Pablo Morales, Carlos Costa, Mario de la Pena, and Armando Alejandre, the victims of the attack.

(3) The Congress urges the President to seek, in the International Court of Justice, indictment for this act of terrorism by Fidel Castro.

As of today, the International Court of Justice has not been capable of bringing Castro to trial.

The Wide-Reaching Arms of the Act

The Helms-Burton Act tries to cover a lot of ground. It addresses concerns about the Jaragua Nuclear Plant near Cienfuegos, Cuba. The construction of this plant, at the time of the writing of the act, had been halted since 1992, following the evaporation of critical funds and support from the Soviet Union. The act further notes that inspections had raised serious concerns about the quality of construction materials and methods, leading to concerns about the safety of the plant. Images of the nuclear disaster ten years earlier at Chernobyl must have abounded in the minds of the authors, and rightly so. The act brings to light several factors in arguing against reinitiation of construction of this plant, but most of these not as serious as the implied threat of a repeat Chernobyl disaster, with a nuclear fallout that would certainly reach vast numbers of US citizens in the Gulf Coast states and beyond.

Section 113 seeks the extradition of "all persons residing in Cuba who are sought by the United States Department of Justice for crimes committed in the United States." This has been interpreted as seeking the return of the US citizen Robert Vesco to face charges for embezzling millions of dollars in the United States, although it does not mention his name.

But the act's one glaring omission is that nowhere within it are means stipulated to directly provide full, adequate, and unencumbered support to achieve this goal [of removing Castro].

The act addresses the exchange of news bureaus, the reinstitution of family remittances and travel to Cuba, the assistance that the United States will provide to the Cuban people, restrictions of Cuban products, restrictions toward financial assistance for projects within Cuba, and many more just as varied issues. The common point between most of those items is that the president is either provided with the opportunity to suspend a portion of the act for up to six months at a time, or that it will only go into effect once the government of Fidel Castro has been removed from office.

The Helms-Burton Act attempted to provide teeth to the embargo, while allowing the logical suspension of key portions to avoid hurting the United States, but the act has served to carry out the agenda of Castro despite its intentions.

Time and again the act calls, directly or indirectly, for the removal of Fidel Castro and his regime as a key condition for the lifting of sanctions, or for allowing assistance to be provided to the Cuban people. This is a great idea, one that all of us within the exiled Cuban community, naturalized Americans of Cuban decent, and the majority of American citizens desire. But the act's one glaring omission is that nowhere within it are means stipulated to directly provide full, adequate, and unencumbered support to achieve this goal.

The United States Needs a Wake-Up Call

The US government needs to take a long, hard look at this act, as well as other enacted policies toward Cuba, and come to the realization that the current plan of course has failed, in portions and collectively since the current administration has a tendency to "stay the course, come hell or high water," as demonstrated in Iraq and elsewhere, the much-needed changes that would either modify the embargo to placate concerns of the international community and thus bring it onboard, or that would eliminate the embargo for another course of action, are changes that will likely continue to elude us, thereby further postponing democracy in Cuba.

7

The Embargo Against Cuba Helped Castro Justify Oppression

Edward J. González

Edward J. González is a first-generation Cuban American.

*Cubans, both in the United States and in Cuba, need to take re-
sponsibility for leading the way toward change in Cuba. The
United States has repeatedly shown that it will not act on behalf
of Cubans. In fact, the U.S. embargo has done nothing but
present Fidel Castro with a means for justifying human rights
violations throughout his regime. Although the United States
could intervene on behalf of the Cuban people, it has chosen to
do nothing and maintains the failed embargo only to give the
appearance of holding a hard line against Cuba.*

Elpidio, as he prefers to be addressed by friends and families, has been a close personal friend of my parents since
many years before I was born. A Cuban-born lawyer, he was
also affectionately called "a walking encyclopedia" by his
friends, due to his constant and voracious thirst for knowledge, coupled with ease of providing and sharing his knowledge with anyone who cared to ask. All you had to do was be
willing to listen. "*Oigo.*". . .

This is the "Henry Kissinger" of the exiled Cuban community, as he has been called. He is not interested in material
wealth; for other than his family, wealth for him is knowledge.

Elpidio has dedicated his adult life to battling the injustices of Castro's regime. For this he had to flee the island, arriving in Miami on June 12, 1966. A well-educated man, the son of an educator who wrote textbooks still used in Cuba to teach children to read and write, Elpidio removed his children from the Cuban public schools six years before he was able to leave, due to his dismay caused by the indoctrination and misinformation that was being forced into their young minds. Elpidio's love for knowledge and books is such that at great personal risk he smuggled out of Cuba a full set of the encyclopedia *Espesa*, the Spanish equivalent of *Britannica*, just prior to his departure, rather than leave them behind and be destroyed as "counter-revolutionary" material.

The embargo is a U.S. political tool, no more, no less.

Effects of the Embargo

As we discuss the embargo and its affect on his life, his voice remains clear and strong. He has studied this subject in detail, and is very informative. Part of his life now revolves around the weekly political newsletter he publishes and cowrites. His replies are intelligent and well thought out, delivered in a rational manner, as you'd expect an intellectual university professor to do, at times peppered with Latin phrases and colloquialisms, but never an obscenity. In response to why he felt he had to leave Cuba, he replies: "*Vis compulsiva.*" He "needed to." . . .

When asked to describe himself as pro- or anti-embargo, he firmly replies: "I fight [Fidel] Castro." He proceeds to explain that for him the embargo is a U.S. political tool, no more, no less. Cubans need to fight Castro with whatever means available to them, but the embargo is a U.S. problem, not a Cuban problem. "The solution to the Cuban problem of Fidel will have to come from us, the Cubans, exiled or not. For us to think that the U.S. or any other nation is going to solve our problem is a big mistake, one that I fight against constantly." He describes how every election year, "presidents and other political hopefuls come to Miami, to Calle Ocho, drink Cuban coffee, give speeches, maybe even play a little dominoes. And they all do the same, they say 'Viva Cuba Libre!' so we give them our support, they are elected, and we don't see them or hear those words again for another four years." He easily accepts this as part of the way of political life in the US, something that reinforces his belief that change in Cuba will come only from Cubans. There is no anger in his voice, no resentment. This is just one more fact in the professor's lecture, the way it is.

The Embargo's History

During a subsequent visit and interview with Elpidio at his home, he explains,

> [Dwight D.] Eisenhower established the embargo for political reasons in 1960. This was an executive decision; one done without the American Congress, although eventually in 1996 Congress formalized the embargo through the Helms-Burton Act. The Cuban revolutionary government was less than two years old at that time when relationships were severed. Initially sanctions were imposed in an effort to [get] Fidel Castro to agree with requests by the United States government. The acts committed by Fidel Castro against American interests in Cuba were further aggravated by this being in the midst of the Cold War between the United States and the then Soviet Union, a formidable adversary that was strategically poised to gain control of Cuba. Or so they thought. Castro is smart, was astute in the manner he played the Soviets, although it was at some cost to him. As Castro was obligated to cease commerce with the United States, he had to turn and depend on the Soviets. This was most evident in the sugar industry, where without the American technology he had to submit to the substandard Soviet hardware and equipment. Even then, he never did ca-

pitulate one hundred percent to the Soviets. As the embargo limited Castro's options, he sought ways to circumvent it while attaining a certain independence from the Soviet Union.

Elpidio pauses, his voice still strong, and offers some Cuban coffee, which his wife quickly prepares and serves before a chance to decline is tended. He frequently pauses to patiently make sure I am following his train of thought and reasoning.

"With the embargo in place, the Soviets thought they would be able to take advantage of it to control Cuba. But Castro managed to stay ahead of them, and in 1964 placed the entire communist party on trial, through the trial of one man, of Mario Rodriguez, a minor individual associated with the communist party in Cuba, that was controlled by the Soviets. Through this means it became obvious that Castro was willing to establish a Castro communism, not just communism. The Soviets realized that Cuba was a great prize for them, so in the end they put up with a lot from Castro."

Human Rights in Cuba

"So, although the embargo caused Castro to have to purchase the inferior Soviet products rather than the American ones he desired, Castro also realized that having the embargo in place would allow him to further tighten his controlling grip on the Cuban populace. One means of doing this was by establishing the *Comite de la Revolución* (Committee of the Revolution) and [using] it as a means to suppress human rights and stay in power."

For Fidel Castro the embargo was the best thing that could have happened to him. It insured that he would remain in power and maintain his [regime].

As we sip the potent coffee offered in diminutive cups, as is customary, Elpidio proceeds to discourse on the rights trampled in Cuba subsequent to the implementation of the embargo: "These were rights taken for granted in democratic countries: the right to communicate, the right to assemble, to live where you wish to live, the right to decide for yourself; these and others were suppressed by Castro. This would never happen in a country such as the United States, for there is legislation guaranteeing rights and giving recourse against abuses by the government. As an individual you have acquired rights . . . but human rights are those rights recognized as a part of humanity, of being a human, a more precise and precious right that has been incorporated recently into the constitutions of most modern countries. For Fidel Castro the embargo was the best thing that could have happened to him. It insured that he would remain in power and maintain his [regime]." . . .

In March 1962, while Elpidio was still living in Cuba, hoping against all indicators that his beloved Cuba would be able to right its course and remove the threat to the nation of Castro, Castro imposed the ration card. For Elpidio, that the ration cards came as an alleged result of the embargo is a point he wishes to emphasize: "*Anote, que esto es importante joven.*" (Make a note of this young man, for it is important.) "The ration card was imposed as a further method—another tool to control the people. It was not needed as a result of the embargo, as Castro claimed, but was imposed as a means to further control Cubans in a more efficient manner, while suppressing more of their rights, their rights to acquire food and goods. Castro [convinced] Cubans that the ration cards were needed, as the Americans had imposed an embargo and goods were scarce."

The recollection of these injustices causes Elpidio's face to become flushed with anger and sadness. For him the manipulation of the embargo by Castro, for the sole purpose of controlling the Cuban people and stripping them of their human rights, was an evil act, a travesty.

"It is amazing that so many nations, the United States, Canada, European states, and others that profess to be stalwart defenders of human rights, can sit idly and watch the abuses committed in Cuba without so much as a peep." This is said almost as a whisper, a rare moment when Elpidio briefly shows weariness.

The embargo serves as an excuse for Castro to hide behind and justify in certain ways that the responsibility is not his for the difficulties suffered by the people.

The Embargo Benefits Castro

Elpidio was surprised initially when Castro opted for the dollarization of Cuba's economy. "Fidel Castro must have done this for financial reasons, not economic. Yet how can a country claim to be a sovereign state when it does not own its own currency?" Elpidio launches into a lengthy lesson on how the G-7 [Britain, Canada, France, Germany, Italy, Japan, United States] nations, initially G-5 [France, Germany, Japan, United Kingdom, United States] following World War II, moved to have currencies' value declared by fiat and tied into the GNP of each nation. Elpidio asks that "Who can establish a value of Cuba's pesos if it is using the currency of another country and Castro will not divulge Cuba's actual GNP? Castro can continue to claim economic hardships, apply for international monetary assistance, all the while not divulging the true extent of his disastrous fiscal policies." This is seen by Elpidio as another means to control the country further while continuing to use the embargo as an excuse. "Castro benefits well from the embargo. He works hard to put a farcical front to denounce the embargo, all the while making sure not to push that envelope so far that the embargo is actually dismantled. The embargo serves as an excuse for Castro to hide behind and justify in certain ways that the responsibility is not his for the difficulties suffered by the people."

"This advantage allows him to oppress and control the people while entrenching him in power for 47 years, as of December 31, 2006. Castro uses the embargo as he controls. He does not allow people to see and visit with each other, to deal in commerce, or to have access to real information. There is no access to books, no books in circulation, no exchange of ideas, and no true knowledge of what is happening in the world."

Why does the United States not mount a campaign to inform the Cuban people about the embargo and how to change it?

I ask Elpidio if the dissidents in Cuba are perhaps a small counter-measure to this. He does not think that they are truly effective at any level, for "their libraries are like a grain of rice in a sack full of rice; such little information is lost in the vast expanse of misinformation and no information."

"The Cuban system is a closed society . . . needed by Castro to be able to control. It is a system established expressly for centralized power, and it needs the embargo to provide the rest of the world, the *come bolas* (fools), the so-called intellectuals, that believe Castro is the victim, and see the embargo as proof of that victimization. The day the embargo ends . . ." Elpidio's voice trails off, but the gleam in his eyes says it all. I hope he will still be here on this earth the day the embargo is gone, and will be able to see the faces of Castro's supporters and the embargo's supporters as they realize that they have been had, one and all, by Castro and by the United States and its embargo.

The Embargo Benefits the United States

The belief that the United States is pursuing its own objectives while stating an altruistic goal of helping the Cuban people with the embargo is evident once more. "Why does the United

States not mount a campaign to inform the Cuban people about the embargo and how to change it?" Elpidio asks rhetorically, and answers, "Because it is for the advantage of the United States to keep this embargo in place and pretend that it is doing something, when in actuality it is doing nothing. Fidel Castro in power helps balance power in the Caribbean basin, and that appears to be a desired objective by the United States, a method of dominating the region while protecting other nations from the threat of Castro's communism."

Yet Elpidio also sees this as a two-way venture that also benefits Castro, allowing him to solidify his grip on power. "The Cuban government in 1934 suppressed the Platt Amendment [part of the Army Appropriations Act, passed in 1901, which stipulated conditions for the withdrawal of U.S. troops from Cuba following the Spanish-American war] along with receiving back from the United States all the bases in occupied in Cuba except for Guantánamo. The United States occupying Guantánamo is good for Castro as it provides an alternative means of communication with the U.S., and can also serve as a method to create further conflict as needed."

This is but one of several agreements that Elpidio points to that show that there is a level of cooperation between Castro and the U.S. that tends to be kept under wraps. "Look at how [Bill] Clinton agreed to return intercepted rafters through Guantánamo. Why? Why did the United States agree to do that? To essentially become the de facto Coast Guard for Cuba? Because it is convenient to United States policies, and the suffering Cubans be damned!"

This is a particular example of the Jekyll and Hyde attitudes that I have also observed of the United States government. I have discussed this with Elpidio and many others, ultimately arriving at the following question: United States officials believe in keeping the embargo intact, are aware of the dismal standard of living for ordinary Cubans, and choose to believe it is a result of the embargo, an embargo placed and enforced by the United States alone, but how does it look to them to have a continued flood of refugees entering the country in a high-risk, high-mortality manner, when the embargo is supposed to help these people?

8

The Travel Ban Was Only a Political Move

Joel Mathis, Mike Shields, and Eric Weslander

Joel Mathis is a "blue" moderator at redblueamerica.com and a former managing editor at Lawrence Journal-World. *Mike Shields is managing editor for Kansas Health Institute and a former city editor at* Lawrence Journal-World. *Eric Weslander is a reporter at* Lawrence Journal-World.

U.S. citizens traveling to Cuba for recreation or other benign purposes are receiving enormous fines for "trading with the enemy" under an old law that had previously lain nearly dormant for almost forty years. It appears the only reason for enforcing the law—and hitting unlicensed but harmless travelers with large penalties—was to help President George W. Bush win the 2004 election. President Bush needed to secure votes in Florida and had been threatened with a loss of support if he did not tighten his stance against Cuba. The travel ban needs to be lifted because it does nothing but further the Castro regime by allowing resentment against the United States to thrive.

Most Americans wouldn't consider them traitors or dangerous. But the [George W.] Bush administration does, and it's going after them.

One of the culprits bagged by the Bush enforcers was a 75-year-old grandmother who thought she was taking a harmless bicyclist's vacation in Cuba. The Bush administration, using a federal law that had been largely ignored for most of its 40-year history and considered by many to be unconstitutional, nailed her for "trading with the enemy."

A Christian fundamentalist from Indiana went to Cuba to deliver Bibles. She was caught and fined for "trading with the enemy." Now, she's worried the Bush administration might come down on other members of her church should she reveal their names.

Across America, including in Lawrence [Kansas], the Bush enforcers are turning up the heat, often years after the violations occurred, on people whose sole crime was traveling to Cuba. In many, if not most, instances the tourists have been charged simply because they admitted to the trips.

"All these people who are getting these fines are truth-tellers," said Sarah Stephens of the Freedom to Travel Project sponsored by the Center for International Policy, which is based in Washington, D.C.

Sneakier visitors to Cuba, including dozens from Lawrence, who took simple steps to avoid leaving a paper trail of their journeys and didn't later confess, have escaped the law's newly wielded hammer.

The Puerto Rican native's crime: going to Cuba to get in touch with his Caribbean roots and visit a girlfriend.

Travel Fines

Bob Augelli, of Lawrence, one of about 2,000 people being pressured by the government for their illegal tourism, has spent the past few months worrying how he would come up with the thousands of dollars in fines he faces for admitting to four trips to Cuba in 1998 and 1999.

More than four years after signing a customs form acknowledging the visits, Augelli was notified last October by the U.S. Treasury Department's Office of Foreign Assets Control that it was serious about collecting $37,000 in fines from him if he refused to settle the agency's claims against him.

"This is certainly a very scary experience—to feel what seems to me the full weight of the government of the U.S. leaning on me," Augelli said, sitting on a sofa beneath a canopy of banana trees growing inside his home off Ninth Street. "It's upsetting. It's stressful. And I think it is particularly stressful in light of the fact that I love my country and I've always considered myself to be a good citizen."

The Puerto Rican native's crime: going to Cuba to get in touch with his Caribbean roots and visit a girlfriend. He came back with the inspiration for an artistic gesture of goodwill for which he later was granted a U.S. license for Cuba travel. That legally sanctioned project, called "Rosa Blanca," took Lawrence landscape muralist Stan Herd to Havana to create a tribute to Cuban poet and patriot Jose Marti.

Marti, the Cuban George Washington, is a hero to Cubans in both Miami and Havana.

"What Bob was trying to do was one more example of folks trying to engage constructively and build a better world," said Bill Martinez of San Francisco, one of Augelli's attorneys. "Rosa Blanca was supposed to be such a universal statement of peace and love."

According to Cuba Travel USA, an estimated 60,000 Americans traveled during 2001 to Cuba illegally.

The Law

The Cuban provisions of the Trading with the Enemy Act became law in 1963, in the wake of the Cuban Missile Crisis. But most U.S. administrations couldn't be bothered to enforce it. For years it has mostly been considered a dead-letter law, enforced inconsistently, if at all, an archaic leftover of the Cold War.

According to the Office of Foreign Assets Control [OFAC], the U.S. Treasury Department agency that enforces the Cuban travel ban, only 188 letters were mailed to travel-ban violators in the last year of the Clinton administration, which took steps that actually encouraged a flood of U.S. tourists to Cuba.

But within months of Bush taking office, almost 500 letters had been sent. And as Bush's first term draws to an end [2004], OFAC's Civil Penalties Division has a docket of nearly 2,000 actions relating to Cuban embargo violations.

According to Cuba Travel USA, an estimated 60,000 Americans traveled during 2001 to Cuba illegally. Among those allowed to legally travel to Cuba and to send money there are Cuban-Americans, the group that is the major political force opposing the right of other Americans to visit the island.

Securing the Election

Prominent—and some unexpected—critics of the hard-line Bush enforcement actions and policies toward Cuba say the only logic to the administration's new zeal in enforcing the old law is that of winning [the 2004] elections.

"This policy is controlled by the president of the U.S. and the political forces around him," said former Kansas congressman and U.S. Agriculture Secretary Dan Glickman. "Look, the president won Florida by 500-some odd votes, and this is going to be another close election. They don't want to lose Florida. This is nothing more than presidential electoral politics."

Glickman is now director of the Institute of Politics at Harvard University's John F. Kennedy School of Government.

The new, tough Cuba line is popular with an influential portion of a tiny, U.S. minority: politically conservative Cuban-Americans, whose passion for unseating Cuban dictator Fidel Castro is undiminished after more than four decades in exile. Supporters of the Cuban embargo say tourist dollars line the pockets of Castro's repressive regime.

South Florida Battleground

"Once that tourist leaves, the people stay," said Mariela Ferretti, a spokeswoman for the Cuban American National Foundation, a Miami-based group that supports the travel ban. "They're the ones who have to face the prisons."

The strongest outpost of the Cuban exile community, which makes up less than one-half of 1 percent of the U.S. population, is the south Florida counties where the 500 votes that decided the 2000 presidential election were cast.

U.S. Sen. Pat Roberts, the Kansas Republican who heads the Senate Intelligence Committee, agreed that Augelli and others caught by the Bush crackdown were victims of Bush family electioneering.

"Two years ago it was the governorship. Four years ago it was the presidential thing. Now, it's the presidential thing again," Roberts told the Journal-World.

The governorship Roberts mentioned was the one successfully sought in Florida by Jeb Bush, George W. Bush's brother.

Ending the Embargo

The hard-line enforcement also comes despite strong evidence most Americans support lifting the ban against Cuba travel. At very least, a majority of their representatives in Congress support removing the ban.

The embargo harms average Cubans and strengthens Castro's hand by allowing mistrust and misinformation about the United States to flourish in Cuba.

In September [2003] the U.S. House approved, 227-188, an amendment suspending enforcement of the travel ban. In November [2003], the Senate followed suit 59-36. But congressional opposition to the travel ban wilted in the face of an expected Bush veto. The Republican leaders of Congress let the amendment die in a conference committee rather than risk a showdown with the president.

Critics say the administration's stance toward Cuba is meant to appease the anti-Castro passions of the Cuban exile community leadership, even though there is evidence Cuban Americans themselves are increasingly divided over the embargo.

Roberts and others argue the embargo harms average Cubans and strengthens Castro's hand by allowing mistrust and misinformation about the United States to flourish in Cuba. It also gives Castro a handy excuse for the island's economic problems. And the embargo, critics say, in slamming the door to Cuba prevents U.S. businesses and agriculture interests from fully exploiting a critical new market in their own back yard. . . .

Florida Threat

Last August [2003] a group of Republican state lawmakers in Florida wrote to Bush warning him that unless he made "substantial progress" toughening the U.S. stance against Cuba, he and other Republicans risked losing Cuban Americans' support in the 2004 elections.

And, warned Florida state Rep. Juan Carlos Planas, Bush "needs to know that unless things change, the support he has gotten in the past will not be there."

Bush apparently got the message.

Two months later in a Rose Garden ceremony, the president announced a commission charged with planning Cuba's "transition" to a free society. He announced an increase in the number of Cuban immigrants allowed into the United States each year. And he promised a tougher travel ban.

"We're cracking down on this deception," Bush said. "I've instructed the Department of Homeland Security to increase inspections of travelers and shipments to and from Cuba. We will enforce the law."

It was about the same time Augelli and hundreds of other Americans began learning the Bush administration meant business. . . .

Bush enforcers are making no apologies for the crackdown, regardless that missionaries and pedal-pushing grandmas are being caught in the net.

9

With Fidel's Resignation, It Is Time to End the Embargo Against Cuba

David R. Henderson

David R. Henderson is an associate professor of economics at the Graduate School of Business and Public Policy and the Naval Postgraduate School and a research fellow with the Hoover Institution. He is also the author of numerous articles and the book The Joy of Freedom: An Economist's Odyssey, *and he is co-author of* Making Great Decisions in Business and Life.

The U.S. embargo against Cuba is not only ineffective but actually aided Castro in building his brutal regime. Over the course of almost fifty years, Castro used the embargo to increase anti–United States sentiment within Cuba and make Cubans more dependent on the government. There is no question that Castro wanted the embargo kept in place, which was further evidenced in the 1996 downing of two American planes by the Cuban air force just days before Congress was to vote on the Helms-Burton Act. Although President Bill Clinton had previously been against it, the embargo-strengthening Helms-Burton Act was easily passed in response to the catastrophe. With Fidel Castro's resignation, the time is once again right for the United States to end the embargo.

Whenever a bloodthirsty dictator resigns or, even better, dies, I pause to celebrate. I would have celebrated at [Adolf] Hitler's death had I been alive then. Ditto [Joseph]

David R. Henderson, "End the Cuban Embargo," *www.antiwar.com*, February 21, 2008. Copyright © 2008 David R. Henderson. Reproduced by permission of the author.

Stalin. And I did celebrate when Mao [Zedong] died. I look forward to Fidel Castro's death. After all the murders he has committed, he deserves it. . . .

At the same time, despite the knee-jerk reaction of the [George W.] Bush administration in favor of keeping the embargo, this is a good time to end the U.S. embargo on Cuba. Actually, it has always been a good time. The case for ending the embargo has little to do with making Americans better off and lots to do with spreading American values—the good ones, not the bad ones—to make Cubans better off, both in their degree of freedom and in their economic well-being. And now that Fidel Castro is officially out of commission, ending the embargo would be easier because the U.S. government would not have to worry so much about saving face.

American leaders did say, loudly and insistently, that Castro must go. And, at the same time, President Bush II strengthened the embargo.

The Moral Case for the Embargo

Let's step back and consider the proponents' case for the embargo. They make two arguments. The first is a straight moral argument: Castro (we need not quibble with whether it's Raúl or Fidel) is an evil man who heads an evil regime. The Castros have murdered many innocent people, stolen a lot of property, and put many innocent people, including homosexuals, in prison. So far, I agree with the argument. But here's the non sequitur: because of all this, the U.S. government should forcibly prevent Americans from trading with Cuba. Why is it a non sequitur? Because for the trade embargo to be a logical response to the vicious facts about the Cuban government, one would have to show that the embargo would speed the end of the Cuban government. No one has done that. Jeff Jacoby, in a 1998 article in the *Boston Globe*, made the moral argument above. He ended his article with the following flourish:

> The key to Cuba's salvation does not lie in constantly attacking U.S. policy. It lies in washing away the corrupt and fetid stain of Fidelismo. The embargo is regrettable and has its costs, but it is not what keeps Cubans on their knees. The dictator is. Instead of harping on the embargo, American leaders should be saying, loudly and insistently, what every Cuban yearns to hear:
>
> "'Castro must go.'"

But notice something interesting. American leaders did say, loudly and insistently, that Castro must go. And, at the same time, President Bush II strengthened the embargo. What happened to Castro? He lasted more years in power. His leaving power had nothing to do with the embargo; it was caused by his bad health. It is possible that Castro's bad health is due to lousy socialized medicine, but, if so, that's more his fault than it is the effect of the embargo. If your moral argument is that a policy must be kept in place to achieve a certain end, and the policy clearly does not achieve that end, aren't you morally obligated to reconsider the policy?

Make the Victims Hurt More

Which brings us to the second argument for the embargo, which seems to go as follows.

By squeezing the Cuban economy enough, the U.S. government can make Cubans even poorer than Fidel Castro has managed to over the past 48 years, through his imposition of Stalin-style socialism. Ultimately, the theory goes, some desperate Cubans will rise up and overthrow Castro.

There are at least three problems with this "make the victims hurt more" strategy. First, it's profoundly immoral. It could succeed only by making average Cubans—already living in grinding poverty—even poorer. Most of them are completely innocent and, indeed, many of them already want to get rid of Castro. And consider the irony: A defining feature of socialism is the prohibition of voluntary exchange between people. Pro-embargo Americans typically want to get rid of socialism in Cuba. Yet their solution—prohibiting trade with Americans—is the very essence of socialism.

The embargo surely makes Cubans somewhat more anti-American than they would be otherwise, and it makes them somewhat more in favor of—or at least less against—Castro.

The Embargo's Failure

The second problem is more practical: It hasn't worked. To be effective, an embargo must prevent people in the target country from getting goods, or at least substantially increase the cost of getting goods. But competition is a hardy weed that shrugs off governmental attempts to suppress it. Companies in many countries, especially Canada, produce and sell goods that are close substitutes for the U.S. goods that can't be sold to Cuba. Wander around Cuba, and you're likely to see beach umbrellas advertising Labatt's beer, McCain's French fries, and President's Choice cola. Moreover, even U.S. goods for which there are no close substitutes are often sold to buyers in other countries, who then resell to Cuba. A layer of otherwise unnecessary middlemen is added, pushing up prices somewhat, but the price increase is probably small for most goods.

Some observers have argued that the very fact that the embargo does little harm means that it should be kept because it's a cheap way for U.S. politicians to express moral outrage against Castro. But arguing for a policy on the grounds that it's ineffective should make people question the policy's wisdom.

Third, the policy is politically effective, but not in the way the embargo's proponents would wish. The embargo surely makes Cubans somewhat more anti-American than they would be otherwise, and it makes them somewhat more in favor of—or at least less against—Castro. Castro has never talked honestly about the embargo: he has always called it a blockade, which it manifestly is not. But he has gotten political mileage by blaming the embargo, rather than socialism, for Cuba's awful economic plight and reminds his subjects ceaselessly that the U.S. government is the instigator. Some Cubans probably believe him.

Moreover, there is another negative political effect. The embargo prohibits Americans, other than journalists, academics, and a few others, from traveling to Cuba. Imagine what would happen if the U.S. government completely ended this restriction. The U.S. dollar, though weak in Europe, is strong in Cuba. Many Americans would travel to Cuba, spending money and showing Cubans what normal Americans can afford. It's true that Raúl Castro, like his brother, would try to control exchange. Currently, foreign investors don't hire Cubans. Instead, Castro has implemented the system that the Nazis used in Poland when Oskar Schindler hired Jews. Rather than paying the Jews, Schindler had to pay the Nazis, who paid the Jews nothing. Rather than hiring Cubans, foreign investors pay the Ministry of Labor, which keeps a large percent of it, and gives the workers a wage comparable to the best they could earn in the Cuban economy. In 2006, incidentally, *Forbes* estimated Fidel Castro's net worth to be a cool $900 million, based on the state-owned companies he controlled for his own purposes.

Although the Cuban government would try to control exchange, it would not be completely successful. There would be all kinds of leakages to normal Cuban citizens. This travel by Americans would not make Cuba as free as, say, Venezuela, but average Cubans would be freer nevertheless. Competing decentralized nodes break down centralized control.

The Conquest of the United States by Cuba

In 1996, far from ending the embargo, the U.S. government moved in the other direction with the Helms-Burton Act, named for then Senator Jesse Helms (R-North Carolina) and then Representative Dan Burton (R-Indiana). Its most controversial provision permits U.S. lawsuits against foreign companies if they use any property in Cuba that was confiscated from U.S. citizens.

To enforce this provision of the Helms-Burton law, the U.S. government makes America off-limits to corporate officers, principals, or shareholders with a controlling interest in firms that profit from confiscated U.S. property in Cuba. The government used the law against a handful of Canadian and Mexican executives. Not just the violators, but also their spouses, minor children, and agents are to be kept out of the U.S. Again, note the irony. One of the most important achievements of free societies—one that distinguishes them most from totalitarian regimes—is that when one family member breaks the law, that person, not the other family members, pays the penalty. Totalitarian governments violate this principle of individual responsibility all the time, and Castro was one of the main such violators left. The U.S. government joined him. Helms and Burton said they wanted to beat Castro. Castro beat them—and us.

I've heard many people claim, correctly, that Castro is evil; I haven't heard many people say that he's stupid.

The more open trade is between Cuba and the rest of the world, the more experience Cubans will have with foreigners and foreign goods. They will learn that they don't have to be poor, that meat once a day doesn't have to be a luxury, and that they don't have to die from socialized medicine. The "dollarization" of the Cuban economy, under which Castro allowed people to exchange dollars for goods, has already started this process. The more dollars that flow into Cuba, even with the nasty government taking a big cut, the less dependent Cubans are on the Cuban government for their daily bread. When President [George W.] Bush reduced the amount Cuban-Americans and other Americans can spend in Cuba from $164 a day to $50 a day, whatever his intention, he made Cubans more dependent on their vicious government.

One piece of evidence that advocates of the embargo must confront is Castro's own actions just before Congress voted on the Helms-Burton Act. Here was a law that President [Bill] Clinton had opposed and that, therefore, faced an uphill battle. Yet on Feb. 24, 1996, just days before the vote, Castro had his air force shoot down two unarmed civilian airplanes piloted by members of the Miami-based exile group Brothers to the Rescue. I've heard many people claim, correctly, that Castro is evil; I haven't heard many people say that he's stupid. Surely he knew that shooting down the plane would cause the Helms-Burton Act to be passed, which is exactly what it did. It seems much more reasonable to assume that Castro wanted the Helms-Burton Act to pass so that he could use it as new ammo for his propaganda.

A Double Standard?

The Bush administration, in wanting to keep the embargo on Cuba, is applying a double standard. Many other governments in the world repress their citizens as much as Cuba's does, or at least have done so in the recent past. Exhibit A is China. But the U.S. government has imposed no embargo on China.

One of the strangest recent arguments for keeping the embargo is that of Henry Louis Gomez. Gomez wrote:

> "For once I'd like for someone to explain how U.S. policy toward Cuba prevents the Castro regime from restoring ba-

sic freedoms? How exactly does the U.S. create a situation in which political opposition in Cuba must be silenced or jailed? The answer is obvious: it doesn't."

Mr. Gomez is absolutely right in one regard. U.S. policy doesn't *prevent* the Castro regime from restoring basic freedoms. It's not as if Fidel and Raúl are looking for ways to restore freedom. But Mr. Gomez is attacking a straw man. The argument that we free-market opponents of the embargo make has never been that the embargo prevents the Cuban government from restoring freedom: the Castros want to keep restrictions on freedom. Our argument, rather, is that the embargo makes it *easier* for the Castros to keep their country repressed. For Mr. Gomez and those who agree with him to make their case, they must confront the point I made above—namely, that Castro is not dumb and, therefore, his shooting down of the airplanes just before Congress voted was his purposeful way of getting Congress to keep and tighten the embargo. . . .

Some advocates of the embargo have pointed out that if full trade relations are resumed between the U.S. and Cuba, then Cuba's government will qualify for U.S. government aid. Such aid would definitely prop up Castro's regime, as similar aid has done for tyrants in Africa and elsewhere. So let's end the embargo and not give foreign aid to Cuba. Will this guarantee that the Castros fade into much deserved oblivion? No it won't. But it will increase the odds.

Cuba Si, Castros No, Embargo No.

10

U.S. Policy May Make the Transition to a Post-Fidel Cuba More Difficult

Mario Loyola

Mario Loyola is a fellow at the Foundation for the Defense of Democracies and a former consultant to the U.S. Defense Department.

Although the United States maintained a tough stance against Cuba since 1960, Fidel Castro was able to thrive for over 40 years in spite of, if not because of, stringent U.S. policies. More than half of Cuban exiles, originally some of the strongest proponents of the U.S. embargo, are reportedly now in favor of seeing the embargo lifted, as are dissident groups in Cuba who continue to call for an end to travel and remittance restrictions. As Cuba begins its transition to a new leader, the United States needs to either change its policy and give hope to Cubans at home and those in exile or risk creating even more instability and conflict in the area.

Commerce Secretary Carlos Gutierrez, who fled the Cuban Revolution at the age of six in 1960, is the [George W.] Bush administration's point man on Cuba policy. He is often asked whether the U.S. embargo is working. "My answer is an emphatic yes," he recently explained. "The embargo has denied Castro resources." Maybe so. But it has also supplied the Castro regime with two things it vitally needs: isolation and a foreign enemy who is not a real threat.

For decades the United States has maintained a policy of complete ostracism of Cuba—no travel, no trade, no remittances, no diplomatic relations. This has not cut the Castro regime off from resources: Cuba receives as much aid from Venezuela's Hugo Chavez as Israel gets from the United States. The policy has accomplished little except to protect the Castro regime from the outside influences that proved fatal to communism in Europe. And it is increasingly poisonous to the interests of the United States.

President [George W.] Bush gave a clue to why this policy survives in his 2007 State of the Union speech when he said, "We will continue to speak out for the cause of freedom in places like Cuba, Belarus, and Burma." Miami representative Ileana Ros-Lehtinen gave the president a beaming thumbs-up, not stopping to think that what defines these three countries as a group is not the repressiveness of their governments (he could then have mentioned China or Saudi Arabia) but rather their strategic irrelevance.

Few Americans are old enough to remember that Cuba was once modern and vibrant, a powerhouse of cultural influence. Modernity was the reason for the revolution. Castro's initial base of support was among the urban middle class—university students, professionals, and small-business owners who wanted democracy. What they got was a cataclysm.

Washington Reacts to Castro

The current U.S. policy towards Cuba was born in the elections of 1960. Castro had been in power nearly two years. Reports of kangaroo courts and summary executions carried live on television horrified the American public, while Castro's fratricidal consolidation of power—along with sweeping seizures of foreign-owned property and military support from the Soviet Union—awoke Washington to a near menace.

In October [1960], John F. Kennedy, the Democratic nominee for president, accused the [Dwight] Eisenhower administration (and by implication his opponent, Vice President Richard Nixon) of permitting the creation of "Communism's first Caribbean base" and allowing Castro to arm himself to the teeth with Soviet weapons. Nixon convinced Eisenhower to react sharply, and, on October 19, the president imposed an embargo on all trade with Cuba. With an indifference that would become characteristic of Washington's attitude, the secretary of commerce, Frederick Henry Mueller, remarked, "If it pushes them into trade with the Communist bloc, that's just too bad." In January, Washington broke off diplomatic relations.

The transformation of Cuba. . .was now complete, with two sets of walls—one erected by Castro to keep everyone in and the other erected by Washington to keep everyone and everything out.

In the months that followed, Castro dramatically increased the seizure of private property and criminalized the free press. When the archbishop of Santiago publicly protested, Castro turned on the church and confiscated all property held by religious organizations. For my grandfather, a pharmacist in the eastern seaside town of Manzanillo who had delivered medicines to Castro's guerrillas in the Sierra Maestra mountains, this was the final straw. Along with hundreds of thousands of his countrymen, he and his family fled to the United States. Betrayed by their former hero, these Cubans would hate Castro with an enduring passion. They would remain implacably opposed to any relaxation of the U.S. embargo.

After the Bay of Pigs invasion failed in 1961, Castro slammed the door shut on the exodus. The transformation of Cuba into a prison was now complete, with two sets of walls—one erected by Castro to keep everyone in and the other erected by Washington to keep everyone and everything out. Cuba's people began their lonely journey into the endless calamities of Castro's dictatorship.

What Castro Wrought

Cuba would now be shaped by Castro's personal—and often sadistic—caprices. When the guerilla leader Huber Matos, the comandante of Camaguey province, attacked the drift towards communism in 1959, Castro sent Matos's best friend to arrest him. (Convicted of treason, Matos spent 20 years in jail.) Castro had no patience for dissent and was always willing to contradict the consensus of his advisers, just to show them that he was in charge. That same summer, a revolutionary tribunal in Santiago acquitted 57 air force officers of the former regime. Castro traveled to the province and personally reversed the verdict, arguing that technicalities could not get in the way of the "revolutionary conscience." The officers were executed en masse by machine gun.

In his 1992 memoir *Before Night Falls*, a horrifying and brilliant chronicle of the Cuban Revolution's first two decades, Reinaldo Arenas recalls that by 1961 basic foodstuffs had disappeared from the markets. Cubans would travel to the new collective farms "begging to buy eggs and chicken; some offered to pay any price for a chicken, but they were denied because a farm 'of the people' couldn't sell to individuals." In 1959, Cuba's per capita GDP was among the highest in Latin America. Just ten years later, Castro's ruinous policies—incompetent even by Communist standards—had made Cuba one of the poorest countries in the world.

Castro's solution was more dictatorship. As Walter Lippmann observed in *The Good Society*, the organizing principle of a Marxist society is not Marxism but militarism. In 1965 Castro launched a plan to increase the sugar harvest to 10 million tons of sugarcane in 1970. Arenas was among the hundreds of thousands of Cubans driven into the field to work the harvest.

The farm was, in reality, an immense military unit. All those who participated in cutting the sugarcane were young recruits who had to work there obligatorily. To enter one of those places was to enter the last circle of hell. . . . I had seen trials in which young men were condemned to twenty and thirty years in prison for the mere fact that on the weekend, they had gone to visit their families, their mothers, their girl-friends.

The effort proved unsustainable. Sugar production began to decline and never stopped. Today, sunk by the fall of the Soviet Union, food production in Cuba is less than half of what it was in 1959, and the sugar harvest is less than a tenth of what it was then. The economy no longer produces much of anything. Forced labor has been replaced by involuntary in-dolence. And escape is all but impossible.

If the administration were really aiming to end commu-nism in Cuba, it would look to the policies that worked against communism elsewhere.

Many Cubans are currently serving long prison sen-tences—generally between 20 and 30 years, often without beds or medical attention—convicted of nothing more than at-tempting "to exit the national territory illegally." Many were also charged with piracy: By law there is no such thing as a private boat in Cuba, so trying to get across the Florida Straits—even if it's in your own fishing boat—is by the government's definition an act of piracy. And if someone should try to escape punishment by claiming to have been an unwilling passenger on your boat, you would be charged with terrorism, a capital offense.

In April 2003, dissidents seized a local ferry and headed north towards the coast of Florida. They ran out of fuel on the high seas, and Cuban forces brought the ferry back. The dissidents were tried for "terrorism, piracy, and attempt to il-legally exit the national territory" in a proceeding that lasted just a few hours. They were executed within days. These horrors are the stuff of daily life in Cuba. As Arenas noted, in a totalitarian society, "Calamities are endless."

Congressional Straitjacket

After the fall of the Soviet Union, the U.S. government moved to liberalize its Cuba policy. The [Bill] Clinton administration relaxed some aspects of the embargo and made it easier to travel there. Republicans in Congress fought these moves tooth-and-nail, drafting the Helms-Burton Act to codify the policy of ostracism. Clinton refused to sign it. But, when a pair of American Cessnas were shot down by the Cuban air force in 1996, he reversed course.

Helms-Burton forbids any dealings with Cuba until the regime meets a lengthy wish list of conditions and until both Fidel Castro and his brother Raul are out of power. The regime has to commit suicide or be overthrown before the United States will deign to have any contact with it. It is the negotiating posture of somebody who has no interest in negotiating.

If the administration were really aiming to end communism in Cuba, it would look to the policies that worked against communism elsewhere. During the Cold War, we had diplomatic relations with every country in the Warsaw Pact. We started extending large loans to the Soviet Union in the 1970s and made trade a cornerstone of China policy from the moment of Nixon's opening. One problem facing the Polish Communist regime in the 1980s was the fact that they owed the West $40 billion and were in desperate need of debt relief.

Worse still, just as American officials knew in 1960 that the embargo would push Cuba further into the Soviet bloc, they are well aware that the present policy is pushing Cuba into the arms of Venezuela and Iran—more unwillingly.

The Exiles

In the exile community, opposition to Castro was for decades absolute and nonnegotiable. Exiles urging dialogue were silenced through intimidation and terrorism. In Miami, bombings and other violent acts against foreign consulates, travel agencies, and radio stations were dishearteningly routine.

For the Cubans who left during the revolution, the island had simply ceased to exist. Growing up, I knew Cuba only in stories and old pictures. But that has changed. For those Cubans who have arrived in the United States in the last quarter-century, who actually had to live under the Castro regime, Cuba remains very much present, and such exiles are now in the majority in America. The 1980 Mariel boatlift brought 140,000 Cubans to Miami, and another 300,000 have followed under a visa program negotiated by the Clinton administration to try to alleviate the refugee crisis.

The all-or-nothing approach of U.S. policy is increasing the risk that the transition, when it comes, will be violent.

These exiles know that the problems of Cuba go far beyond Castro. Laritza Diversent, a dissident writing from Havana, recently lamented the "prostitution, delinquency, and corruption that have become indispensable means of subsistence." For the new exiles, Cuba's nightmarish privations weigh more than politics; less than half of them support the embargo. Even among exiles who arrived in the early years of the revolution, there is growing frustration with a policy that has never produced any tangible benefit. Carlos Saladrigas, who escaped Cuba in 1961 and is one of the exile community's most successful businessmen, formed the Cuba Study Group in 2000 to examine policy alternatives.

Saladrigas focuses on the fact that dictatorships need legitimacy. "The Communist regime in Cuba," he explains, "has been able to get legitimacy from two sources: the conflict with the United States and the charisma of Fidel." The United States can eliminate the first one whenever it wants, and the second will soon eliminate itself. Saladrigas notes that Raul Castro is in a much weaker position than his brother and will have to base his legitimacy on actual results. That will force him towards reform. And, as Lech Walesa likes to point out, the Communist system is unreformable.

Roots of Hope

Fidel Castro, the immovable ideological core of the Cuban Revolution, is gone from power and will never come back—in a recent interview released by Cuban state television, Castro showed difficulty completing simple sentences. His brother is far less ideological and never contradicts the consensus of his advisers. Meanwhile, behind the aging oligarchs of the Sierra Maestra generation, there is an entire state full of bureaucrats who know that they will live to see the fall of communism in Cuba and have to think about what happens next. Among them are future allies of the United States.

In an echo of perestroika [economic reforms introduced by Mikhail Gorbachev in June 1985] and glasnost [reforms introduced by Mikhail Gorbachev that instituted transparency in Soviet Union government institutions], two words have crept into official propaganda in the last year: "change" and "dialogue." The word "change" has become common on T-shirts and in windows across Cuba, and the regime has reportedly launched a wide-ranging and historic "internal dialogue" on all issues. For the regime to admit that people want change and the freedom to talk about it, necessarily empowers public opinion as a force in opposition to party ideology. This is the process that destroyed the Communist political monopoly in Eastern Europe and in no case did it follow the rigid prescriptions of Helms-Burton.

The all-or-nothing approach of U.S. policy is increasing the risk that the transition, when it comes, will be violent. That terrifies Cuba's dissidents—and poses grave risks for the United States. Instability could further radicalize the regime and open more opportunities for Venezuela and Iran. It could lead to another refugee crisis. Most ominously, Cuba could become a failing state, overrun by armed gangs with ties to drug trafficking and international terrorism, as in much of Central America.

The U.S. government should be negotiating for incremental transition, because even the smallest reforms will fuel popular expectations for more change. In 1992, Carlos Lage, then finance minister and now vice president, spent many months in Europe putting together a package of reforms aimed at encouraging small business. Castro balked on ideological grounds (he could not live with the thought that someone in Cuba might make a profit), but now that he is effectively out of power, Lage is likely to want to try again. The United States can help him: allowing Cuba access to microfinancing (even if that also gives the regime access to more resources) and letting American firms import products manufactured by privately owned businesses there.

The United States should encourage the Cuban regime to talk to dissident leaders such as Osvaldo Paya—but we should listen to them, too. Every major dissident group in Cuba has called for the United States to lift the restrictions on travel and remittances for Cuban exiles. That alone could reduce the terrible isolation in which Cuba's dissidents are now struggling.

Making the exile community a bridge to Cuba would also allow U.S. policy to profit from the work that Carlos Saladrigas and others have done to build consensus for change among Cubans and to prepare for the end of communism—and of exile. With its "Pillars" declaration, Cuban Consensus—an umbrella organization of dissident and exile groups including the once hardline Cuban American National Foundation—has created a framework of reconciliation for the post-Castro era. Student groups in the United States, such as Roots of Hope, are already nourishing contacts with Cuba's largely dissident youth.

Castro so thoroughly ruined Cuba as to make it irrelevant. That irrelevance—and the tragic inertia it has injected into U.S. policy—now protect the regime he is leaving behind. Meanwhile, Cubans continue to suffer silently, knowing that sooner or later something has to change.

11

Ending the Cuban Embargo Could Harm an Ecological Sanctuary

Cornelia Dean

Cornelia Dean is a science staff writer at The New York Times. *She is also an engineering and applied sciences lecturer at Harvard University and the author of* Against the Tide: The Battle for America's Beaches.

Cuba is home to a wide range of animals and plants, including some species found nowhere else on the planet. Once the embargo is lifted, their habitats could be destroyed by builders anxious to develop these beautiful and important landscapes. Meanwhile, current study and attempts to conserve the island are severely limited by the embargo as scientists are hampered by travel restrictions, restrictions on sending much-needed research equipment to Cuba, and even a lack of Internet capability to support research and communication in Cuba. As tourism expands after the embargo is lifted, the very landscape that draws tourists in may be destroyed.

Through accidents of geography and history, Cuba is a priceless ecological resource. That is why many scientists are so worried about what will become of it after Fidel Castro and his associates leave power and, as is widely anticipated, the American government relaxes or ends its trade embargo.

Cuba, by far the region's largest island, sits at the confluence of the Atlantic Ocean, the Gulf of Mexico and the Caribbean Sea. Its mountains, forests, swamps, coasts and marine areas are rich in plants and animals, some seen nowhere else.

Once the embargo ends, the island could face a flood of investors from the United States and elsewhere, eager to exploit those landscapes.

And since the imposition of the embargo in 1962, and especially with the collapse in 1991 of the Soviet Union, its major economic patron, Cuba's economy has stagnated.

Cuba has not been free of development, including Soviet-style top-down agricultural and mining operations and, in recent years, an expansion of tourism. But it also has an abundance of landscapes that elsewhere in the region have been ripped up, paved over, poisoned or otherwise destroyed in the decades since the Cuban revolution, when development has been most intense. Once the embargo ends, the island could face a flood of investors from the United States and elsewhere, eager to exploit those landscapes.

Protecting Cuba's Natural Resources

Conservationists, environmental lawyers and other experts, from Cuba and elsewhere, met last month in Cancun, Mexico, to discuss the island's resources and how to continue to protect them.

Cuba has done "what we should have done—identify your hot spots of biodiversity and set them aside," said Oliver Houck, a professor of environmental law at Tulane University Law School who attended the conference.

In the late 1990s, Mr. Houck was involved in an effort, financed in part by the MacArthur Foundation, to advise Cuban officials writing new environmental laws.

But, he said in an interview, "an invasion of U.S. consumerism, a U.S.-dominated future, could roll over it like a bulldozer" when the embargo ends.

By some estimates, tourism in Cuba is increasing 10 percent annually. At a minimum, Orlando Rey Santos, the Cuban lawyer who led the law-writing effort, said in an interview at the conference, "we can guess that tourism is going to increase in a very fast way" when the embargo ends.

"It is estimated we could double tourism in one year," said Mr. Rey, who heads environmental efforts at the Cuban ministry of science, technology and environment.

About 700 miles long and about 100 miles wide at its widest, Cuba runs from Haiti west almost to the Yucatan Peninsula of Mexico. It offers crucial habitat for birds, like Bicknell's thrush, whose summer home is in the mountains of New England and Canada, and the North American warblers that stop in Cuba on their way south for the winter.

Zapata Swamp, on the island's southern coast, may be notorious for its mosquitoes, but it is also known for its fish, amphibians, birds and other creatures. Among them is the Cuban crocodile, which has retreated to Cuba from a range that once ran from the Cayman Islands to the Bahamas.

Cuba's Diverse Marine Life

Cuba has the most biologically diverse populations of freshwater fish in the region. Its relatively large underwater coastal shelves are crucial for numerous marine species, including some whose larvae can be carried by currents into waters of the United States, said Ken Lindeman, a marine biologist at Florida Institute of Technology.

Dr. Lindeman, who did not attend the conference but who has spent many years studying Cuba's marine ecology, said in an interview that some of these creatures were important commercial and recreational species like the spiny lobster, grouper or snapper.

Like corals elsewhere, those in Cuba are suffering as global warming raises ocean temperatures and acidity levels. And like other corals in the region, they reeled when a mysterious die-off of sea urchins left them with algae overgrowth. But they have largely escaped damage from pollution, boat traffic and destructive fishing practices.

Diving in them "is like going back in time 50 years," said David Guggenheim, a conference organizer and an ecologist and member of the advisory board of the Harte Research Institute, which helped organize the meeting along with the Center for International Policy, a private group in Washington.

In a report last year, the World Wildlife Fund said that "in dramatic contrast" to its island neighbors, Cuba's beaches, mangroves, reefs, seagrass beds and other habitats were relatively well preserved. Their biggest threat, the report said, was "the prospect of sudden and massive growth in mass tourism when the U.S. embargo lifts."

To prepare for that day, researchers from a number of American institutions and organizations are working on ecological conservation in Cuba, including Harte, the Wildlife Conservation Society, universities like Tulane and Georgetown, institutions like the American Museum of Natural History and the New York Botanical Garden, and others. What they are studying includes coral health, fish stocks, shark abundance, turtle migration and land use patterns.

Cuban scientists at the conference noted that this work continued a tradition of collaboration that dates from the mid-19th century, when Cuban researchers began working with naturalists from the Smithsonian Institution. In the 20th century, naturalists from Harvard and the University of Havana worked together for decades.

U.S. Policy Makes Scientific Research More Difficult

But now, they said, collaborative relationships are full of problems. The Cancun meeting itself illustrated one.

"We would have liked to be able to do this in Havana or in the United States," Jorge Luis Fernandez Chamero, the director of the Cuban science and environment agency and leader of the Cuban delegation, said through a translator in opening the meeting. "This we cannot do." While the American government grants licenses to some (but not all) American scientists seeking to travel to Cuba, it routinely rejects Cuban researchers seeking permission to come to the United States, researchers from both countries said.

So meeting organizers turned to Alberto Mariano Vazquez De la Cerda, a retired admiral in the Mexican navy, an oceanographer with a doctorate from Texas A & M and a member of the Harte advisory board, who supervised arrangements for the Cuban conferees.

The travel situation is potentially even worse for researchers at state institutions in Florida. Jennifer Gebelein, a geographer at Florida International University who uses global positioning systems to track land use in Cuba, told the meeting about restrictions imposed by the Florida Legislature, which has barred state colleges from using public or private funds for travel to Cuba.

As a result of this move and federal restrictions, Dr. Gebelein said "we're not sure what is going to happen" with her research program.

American scientists, foundations and other groups are ready to help with equipment and supplies but are hampered by the embargo.

The Cuban Government Hampers Research Efforts

On the other hand, John Thorbjarnarson, a zoologist with the Wildlife Conservation Society, said that he had difficulty obtaining permission from Cuba to visit some areas in that country, like a habitat area for the Cuban crocodile near the Bay of Pigs.

"I have to walk a delicate line between what the U.S. allows me to do and what the Cubans allow me to do," said Dr. Thorbjarnarson, who did not attend the conference. "It is not easy to walk that line."

But he had nothing but praise for his scientific colleagues in Cuba. Like other American researchers, he described them as doing highly competent work with meager resources. "They are a remarkable bunch of people," Dr. Thorbjarnarson said, "but my counterparts make on average probably less than $20 a month."

American scientists, foundations and other groups are ready to help with equipment and supplies but are hampered by the embargo. For example, Maria Elena Ibarra Martin, a marine scientist at the University of Havana, said through a translator that American organizations had provided Cuban turtle and shark researchers with tags and other equipment. They shipped it via Canada.

Another thorny issue is ships.

"If you are going to do marine science, at some point you have to go out on a ship," said Robert E. Hueter, who directs the center for shark research at the Mote Marine Laboratory in Sarasota, Fla., and attended the Cancun meeting.

But, he and others said, the United States government will not allow ships into American ports if they have recently been in Cuban waters in the previous six months, and the Cuban government will not allow American research vessels in Cuban waters.

One answer might be vessels already in Cuba, but nowadays they are often tied up in tourism-related efforts, Cubans at the Cancun meeting said.

And even with a ship, several American researchers at the conference said, it is difficult to get Cuban government permission to travel to places like the island's northwest coast, the stretch closest to the United States. As a result, that region is the least-studied part of the Cuban coast, Dr. Guggenheim and others said.

Additional Factors Inhibiting Research

Another big problem in Cuba is the lack of access to a source of information researchers almost everywhere else take for granted: the Internet.

Critics blame the Castro government, saying it limits access to the Internet as a form of censorship. The Cuban government blames the embargo, which it says has left the country with inadequate bandwidth and other technical problems that require it to limit Internet access to people who need it most.

In any event, "we find we do not have access," Teresita Borges Hernandez, a biologist in the environment section of Cuba's science and technology ministry, said through a translator. She appealed to the Americans at the meeting to do "anything, anything to improve this situation."

Dr. Guggenheim echoed the concern and said even telephone calls to Cuba often cost as much as $2 a minute. "These details, though they may seem trite," he said, "are central to our ability to collaborate."

As Cuba becomes an increasing popular tourist resort . . . we don't want to see and they don't want to see the same mistakes, where you literally love something to death.

Dr. Gebelein and several of the Cubans at the meeting said that some American Web sites barred access to people whose electronic addresses identify them as Cuban. She suggested that the group organize a Web site in a third country, a site where they could all post data, papers and the like, and everyone would have access to it.

Preparing for Cuba's Future

For Dr. Guggenheim, the best lessons for Cubans to ponder as they contemplate a more prosperous future can be seen 90 miles north, in the Florida Keys. There, he said, too many people have poured into an ecosystem too fragile to support them.

"As Cuba becomes an increasingly popular tourist resort," Dr. Guggenheim said, "we don't want to see and they don't want to see the same mistakes, where you literally love something to death."

But there are people skeptical that Cuba will resist this kind of pressure. One of them is Mr. Houck.

The environmental laws he worked on are "a very strong structure," he said, "But all laws do is give you the opportunity to slow down the wrong thing. Over time, you can wear the law down."

That is particularly true in Cuba, he said, "where there's no armed citizenry out there with high-powered science groups pushing in the opposite direction. What they lack is the counter pressure of environmental groups and environmental activists."

As Mr. Rey and Daniel Whittle, a lawyer for Environmental Defense, put it in the book *Cuban Studies 37*, "policymaking in Cuba is still centralized and top down." But, they wrote, "much can be done to enhance public input in policymaking."

Mr. Rey said in the interview that Cubans must be encouraged to use their environmental laws. By "some kind of cultural habit," he said, people in Cuba rarely turn to the courts to challenge decisions they dislike.

"There's no litigation, just a few cases here and there," Mr. Rey said. "In most community situations if a citizen has a problem he writes a letter. That's O.K., but it's not all the possibilities."

Mr. Rey added, "We have to promote more involvement, not only in access to justice and claims, but in taking part in the decision process."

"I know the state has a good system from the legislative point of view," Mr. Rey said. But as he and Mr. Whittle noted in their paper, "the question now is whether government leaders can and will do what it takes to put the plan on the ground."

12

Agricultural Trade Is Not Likely to Increase Under a New Cuban Leader

Ross Korves

Ross Korves is an economic policy analyst working primarily on trade issues.

The embargo plays a small role in limiting trade to Cuba. The population is too small and incomes in Cuba are too low for the food demand to increase even if the embargo were lifted. Economic reforms in Cuba would have a greater effect on increasing trade with the United States than lifting the embargo.

The ongoing health problems of the current 81-year-old President of Cuba Fidel Castro has raised optimism about the potential for U.S. agricultural trade with Cuba in the years ahead. The close proximity of Cuba puts the U.S. in a strong position to increase trade, but the more important issue is the economic policies of a post-Castro government.

Trade Potential

Cuba is a relatively small market with a population of 11.4 million people. For comparison, the island country of Taiwan has 22.9 million people, Hong Kong has 6.9 million and Singapore has 4.5 million. Its land area of 42,800 square miles is slightly smaller than Pennsylvania, which has a population of

Ross Korves, "Agricultural Trade with Cuba in the Post-Castro Era," *Truth about Trade and Technology*, December 22, 2006. Copyright © 2006. Reproduced by permission. www.truthabouttrade.org

12.4 million. Cuba has a GDP of $1,500 per capita on an economic trade basis, but $3,500 on a purchasing power parity (PPP) basis because many goods and services are subsidized by the government. Again for comparison, Hong Kong's GDP on a PPP basis is $34,000 and Singapore's is $28,600. Three-fourths of the labor force is employed by the government. The economy is still recovering from a severe recession from 1989 to 1993 caused by the withdrawal of subsidies by the former Soviet Union.

About 28 percent of Cuba's land is arable. Agriculture is 5.5 percent of GDP, but has 21 percent of the labor force, and 30 percent of the population lives in rural areas. Sugar production, once the mainstay of agriculture, has declined from 8 million tons in 1989 to 1.5 million tons in 2006. Citrus production was promoted as an alternative to sugar and prospered during the 1970s and 1980s with large shipments to the Soviet Union and other Eastern European countries. Those exports collapsed with the ending of subsidies, and Cuba has been forced to ship products to the competitive EU [European Union] markets.

U.S. agricultural exports to Cuba were $343.2 million in fiscal year 2006.

Current Trade with the United States

Despite the general U.S. trade embargo against Cuba begun 45 years ago, cash sales of food are permitted under the Trade Sanctions Reform and Export Enhancement Act of 2000 and the FY 2001 agricultural appropriations act. Cuba imports food to provide a minimum diet for the people, and U.S. commodities are competitively priced with low transportation costs. The Food and Agriculture Organization of the UN (FAO) reports that malnutrition among children in Cuba is relatively low for a developing country at just under 5 percent. About 9 percent of women and 6 percent of men are considered to be chronically energy deficient, while 37 percent of women and 32 percent of men are overweight.

U.S. agricultural exports to Cuba were $343.2 million in fiscal year 2006. Just over half, $175.4 million, were bulk commodities with course grains at $50.5 million, rice $43.6 million, wheat $43.3 million, soybeans $22.6 million, and pulses $14.9 million. The remaining amount was split between intermediate products at $84.3 million and consumer-oriented products at $83.5 million. The intermediate products were dominated by soybean oil at $38.6 million and soybean meal at $30.4 million. Poultry meat exports of $40 million accounted for almost half of the consumer-oriented products followed by dairy products at $24.2 million and red meat at $15.5 million.

If a new government reformed basic political structures and allowed freedoms similar to the U.S., but did not make economic policy reforms, the market for food would still not grow.

According to FAO data, total Cuban agricultural imports in 2004, the latest year available, were $927 million. In fiscal year 2004 USDA data show the U.S. exported $400 million of agricultural products to Cuba, implying a market share of about 40 percent. Total agricultural exports from Cuba in 2004 according to FAO were $620 million, with sugar at $349 million, cigars at $129 million, alcoholic beverages at $33 million, orange juice at $21 million and grapefruit juice at $17 million.

Trade May Not Increase Even if the Embargo Is Lifted

If President [Fidel] Castro were no longer in power, but there were no changes in political and economic policies, U.S. agricultural exports to Cuba would change little, if any, with or without the embargo. Cuban incomes would remain too low for greater demand for food to develop.

If a new government reformed basic political structures and allowed freedoms similar to the U.S., but did not make economic policy reforms, the market for food would still not grow. Cuba has hard currency foreign debt estimated at $12 billion and does not qualify for lending by institutions like the World Bank because it defaulted on its debt in 1986. It is rated as a poor investment risk and has to pay double digit interest rates on borrowings.

There is economic hope if economic policy reforms are implemented. Nickel is the biggest export item estimated at $1.0 billion in 2005. Other export items include sugar, tobacco, fish, medical products, citrus and coffee.

Tourism as a Solution

The current government has discovered tourism as a major economic force for growth and source of hard currency to pay for imports. Tourist visits totaled 2.3 million in 2005 and generated over $2.0 billion in revenue. Also, funds transferred from Cubans living outside the country, mostly in the U.S., produce $600 million to $1.0 billion per year in hard currencies.

Despite the hard currency debt overhang, an economic policy based on economic freedom would attract outside capital to the country. New investments could rebuild the citrus industry, and the U.S would become a major market for the output. The tourist industry would also attract new investments. These would be engines of economic growth that are necessary to increase incomes to improve the demand for food.

Increasing food demand to the level of other economically successful small nations will not be a quick process, but U.S. producers should not ignore the market. As small countries like Taiwan with U.S. agricultural imports of $2.4 billion per year have shown, economic growth increases demand for the quantity and variety of food and increases trade.

Organizations to Contact

The editors have compiled the following list of organizations concerned with the issues debated in this book. The descriptions are derived from materials provided by the organizations. All have publications or information available for interested readers. The list was compiled on the date of publication of the present volume; the information provided here may change. Be aware that many organizations take several weeks or longer to respond to inquiries, so allow as much time as possible.

The Association for the Study of the Cuban Economy (ASCE)
P.O. Box 28267, Washington, DC   20038-8267
e-mail: asce@ascecuba.org
Web site: http://lanic.utexas.edu/project/asce

The ASCE is a non-profit and non-political professional organization incorporated in the state of Maryland in 1990. Affiliated with the American Economic Association and the Allied Social Sciences Association of the United States, ASCE maintains professional contacts with social scientists throughout the world interested in engaging in scholarly discussion and research on Cuba and its comparative development. The ASCE regularly publishes a newsletter.

Center for a Free Cuba (CFC)
1320 19th Street, NW, Suite 600, Washington, DC   20036
(202) 463-8430 • fax: (202) 463-8412
e-mail: freecuba@cubacenter.org
Web site: www.cubacenter.org

The Center for a Free Cuba (CFC) is an independent, non-partisan institution dedicated to promoting human rights and a transition to democracy and the rule of law on the island. Established in November 1997, the center gathers and disseminates information about Cuba and Cubans to the media,

NGOs, and the international community and assists the people of Cuba through its information outreach and humanitarian programs on the island. The center publishes a monthly report, "This Month in Cuba," focusing on political, economic, and social issues in Cuba.

The Center for International Policy's Cuba Program
1717 Massachusetts Avenue, NW, Suite 801
Washington, DC   20036
(202) 232-3317 • fax: (202) 232-3440
e-mail: cip@ciponline.org
Web site: www.ciponline.org/cuba

Under the direction of Wayne S. Smith, former chief of the U.S. Interests Section in Havana, the Center for International Policy's Cuba Program seeks to bring about a more sensible U.S. policy toward Cuba. The Web site includes several policy reports on United States–Cuba relations.

The Cuba Academic Alliance
The Center for Cross-Cultural Study, 446 Main Street
Amherst, MA   01002
(413) 256-0011 • fax: (413) 256-1968
Web site: www.CubaAcademicAlliance.org

The Cuba Academic Alliance is an informal but focused group of academic institutions organized to respond to the new restrictions imposed by the U.S. government on educational travel and exchange programs to Cuba. Members share information about changes to the rules that could affect U.S. academic programs, and the Web site includes updated information about educational travel.

Cuban American Alliance Education Fund (CAAEF)
1010 Vermont Avenue, NW, Suite 620
Washington, DC   20005
(805) 627-1959 • fax: (805) 627-1959
email: caaef@hughes.net
Web site: www.cubamer.org

The CAAEF is a national network of Cuban Americans formed to educate the public on issues related to hardships resulting from current United States–Cuba relations. The alliance is a vehicle for the development of mutually beneficial engagements that promote understanding and human compassion. The Web site maintains links to recent news articles about Cuba.

Cuban American National Council (CNC)
1223 SW 4 Street, Miami, FL   33135
(305) 642-3484 • fax: (305) 642-9122
Web site: www.cnc.org

The CNC is a non-profit organization providing human services to persons in need from all racial and ethnic groups. CNC assists individuals to become self-reliant and builds bridges among America's diverse communities. The council's policy center publications include a textbook, research monographs, issue briefs, seminar abstracts, and the CNC newsletter, *The Council Letter.*

The Cuban American National Foundation (CANF)
1312 SW 27 Avenue, Miami, FL   33145
(305) 592-7768 • fax: (305) 592-7889
e-mail: hq@canf.org
Web site: www.canf.org

The CANF is a non-profit organization dedicated to advancing freedom and democracy in Cuba. Established in Florida in 1981, CANF is the largest Cuban organization in exile, with thousands of members across the United States and other countries, representing a cross section of the Cuban exile community as well as friends of Cuban freedom from around the world. The Web site contains a numerous articles on the U.S. policy on Cuba.

Cuban and Caribbean Studies Institute
Caroline Richardson Building, New Orleans, LA   70118-5698
(504) 862-8629 • fax: (504) 862-8678

e-mail: cuba@tulane.edu
Web site: www.cuba.tulane.edu

The Cuban and Caribbean Studies Institute, a part of Tulane's Stone Center for Latin American Studies, is responsible for the organization of a variety of lectures, performances, courses, symposia, and other programs aimed at promoting a true academic and cultural exchange between Cuba and the United States. Since its origination, the institute has also led an annual summer study session in Cuba, which provides students with a rare opportunity to study and live in Havana, Cuba.

Cuban Research Institute (CRI)

University Park, DM 353, Miami, FL   33199
(305) 348-2894 • fax: (305) 348-3593
Web site: http://lacc.fiu.edu/cri

The CRI is the nation's leading institute for research and academic programs on Cuban and Cuban American issues and is supported by the Latin American and Caribbean Center at Florida International University. The CRI hosts an international conference and has sponsored numerous publications.

The Free Cuba Foundation

Florida International University, Graham Center 340
Miami, FL   33199
(305) 595-3346
e-mail: fcf@fiu.edu
Web site: www.fiu.edu/~fcf

The Free Cuba Foundation is a non-profit, and non-partisan organization whose purpose is to work toward the establishment of an independent and democratic Cuba using nonviolent means. The Web site provides information on the situation inside of Cuba and the international community's relationship with the island and includes links to current articles on Cuba.

Human Rights Watch, Cuba
1630 Connecticut Avenue, NW, Suite 500
Washington, DC   20009
(202) 612-4321 • fax: (202) 612-4333
e-mail hrwdc@hrw.org
Web site: www.humanrightswatch.org

Human Rights Watch is dedicated to protecting the human rights of people around the world to prevent discrimination, uphold political freedom, protect people from inhumane conduct in wartime, and bring offenders to justice. Human Rights Watch investigates and exposes human rights violations and holds abusers accountable. The Web site includes an overview of human rights issues in Cuba and numerous other press releases, letters, and articles regarding human rights in Cuba.

Institute for Cuban and Cuban-American Studies (ICCAS)
1531 Brescia Avenue, P.O. Box 248174, Coral Gables, FL
   33124-3010
(305) 284-2822 • fax: (305) 284-4875
e-mail: iccas@miami.edu
Web site: www6.miami.edu/iccas/iccas.htm

The ICCAS is part of the University of Miami. ICCAS serves as a world-class academic center for the research and study of Cuban and Cuban American topics. It organizes seminars and lectures, publishes academic research, and offers a special summer program on Cuba for U.S. and foreign students.

International Committee for Democracy in Cuba (ICDC)
Sokolska 18, 120 00, Praha 2
   Czech Republic
+420 226 200 462 • fax: +420 226 200 401
e-mail: icdc@peopleinneed.cz
Web site: www.icdcprague.org

The ICDC was created by prominent international political figures, diplomats and intellectuals from across Europe, the United States, and Latin America who want to show political solidarity with fellow democracy activists in Cuba and channel economic support to Cuba's democratic opposition. ICDC's members have lobbied for political policies within national, regional, and international government bodies that will protect Cuban dissidents, assist human rights initiatives, and call for more consistent approaches to dealing with the Castro regime. The Web site contains several documents on issues related to international relations with Cuba.

Latin America Working Group (LAWG)
424 C Street NE, Washington, DC   20002
(202) 546-7010
e-mail: lawg@lawg.org
Web site: www.lawg.org

The LAWG is one of the nation's longest standing coalitions dedicated to foreign policy. The Latin America Working Group and its sister organization, the Latin America Working Group Education Fund, carry out the coalition's mission to encourage U.S. policies toward Latin America that promote human rights, justice, peace, and sustainable development, including such policies toward Cuba. LAWG publishes the *Advocate*, which is also available on the Web site.

Washington Office on Latin America (WOLA), Cuba
1630 Connecticut Avenue, NW, Suite 200
Washington, DC   20009
(202) 797-2171 • fax: (202) 797-2172
Web site: www.wola.org

WOLA is committed to advancing human rights, democratic institutions, citizen participation, and equitable economic development in Latin America. WOLA publishes a number of resource guides on Cuba, and the Web site contains links to current articles on Cuba.

Bibliography

Books:

Aviva Chomsky and Pamela Maria Smorkaloff, eds.

The Cuban Reader: History, Culture, Politics. Durham, NC: Duke University Press, 2003.

Richard Gott

Cuba: A New History. New Haven, CT: Yale University Press, 2005.

Brian Latell

After Fidel, Updated Edition: Raul Castro and the Future of Cuba's Revolution. New York: Palgrave Macmillan, 2007.

Jeanne Parr Lemkau and David L. Strug

Love, Loss and Longing: The Impact of U.S. Travel Policies on Cuban-American Families. Washington, DC: Latin American Working Group Education Fund, 2007.

Geraldine Lievesley

The Cuban Revolution: Past, Present and Future Perspectives. New York: Palgrave Macmillan, 2004.

Marifeli Perez-Stable, ed.

Looking Forward: Comparative Perspectives on Cuba's Transition. Notre Dame, IN: University of Notre Dame Press, 2007.

Isaac Saney

Cuba: A Revolution in Motion. London: Zed Books, 2004.

Rosemarie Skaine

The Cuban Family: Custom and Change in an Era of Hardship. Jefferson, NC: McFarland, 2004.

Clifford L. Staten   *The History of Cuba*. New York: Palgrave Macmillan, 2005.

Periodicals:

Ernesto F.   "Changing U.S. Cuba Policy," *Society*,
Betancourt   July–August 2006.

Douglas A. Borer   "Rethinking the Cuban Embargo: An
and James D.   Inductive Analysis," *Foreign Policy*
Bowen   *Analysis*, April 2007.

Jorge Castaneda   "Ending the Cuban Exception," *News-
                      week International*, March 10, 2008.

Joseph Contreras   "Island of Failed Promises," *News-
                      week*, March 3, 2008.

The Economist   "The Americans Have Come; Cuba
                      and the United States," January 4,
                      2003.

Richard Garfield   "Health Care in Cuba and the Ma-
                      nipulation of Humanitarian Impera-
                      tives," *The Lancet*, September 11,
                      2004.

Marc Lacey   "Report Finds U.S. Agencies Dis-
                      tracted by Focus on Cuba," *The New
                      York Times*, December 19, 2007.

Anatol Lieven   "It's Time to Trade with Cuba;
                      Capitalism's Appeal," *International
                      Herald Tribune*, April 26, 2007.

Sheryl L. Lutjens   "National Security, the State, and the Politics of U.S.-Cuba Educational Exchange," *Latin American Perspectives*, September 2006.

Ana Menendez   "Greed Lays Bare the Embargo's Cruel Hypocrisy," *Miami Herald*, June 10, 2007.

Marty Roney   "U.S. Exports to Cuba Take Off," *USA Today*, July 30, 2007.

Joseph Scarpaci, Jr.   "Photojournal: Cuba," *Focus on Geography*, Winter 2007.

Alicia Shepard   "A Crackdown Leading Nowhere," *Washington Post*, July 13, 2003.

Michael Shermer   "Why We Should Trade with Cuba," *The Huffington Post*, January 23, 2008. www.huffingtonpost.com/michael-shermer

Lissa Weinmann   "Washington's Irrational Cuba Policy," *World Library Journal*, Spring 2004.

Index